WHAT IS THE BOOK OF REVELATION?

Kids' Guides to God's Word Series

What Is the Book of Genesis?
What Is the Book of Exodus?
What Is the Book of Leviticus?
What Is the Book of Numbers?
What Is the Book of Deuteronomy?
What Is the Book of Joshua?
What Is the Book of Judges?
What Is the Book of Ruth?
What Is the Book of 1 Samuel?
What Is the Book of 2 Samuel?
What Is the Book of 1 Kings?
What Is the Book of 2 Kings?
What Are the Books of 1–2 Chronicles?
What Are the Books of Ezra & Nehemiah?
What Is the Book of Esther?
What Is the Book of Job?
What Is the Book of Psalms?
What Is the Book of Proverbs?
What Is the Book of Ecclesiastes?
What Are the Books of Song of Songs &
Lamentations?
What Is the Book of Isaiah?
What Is the Book of Jeremiah?
What Is the Book of Ezekiel?
What Is the Book of Daniel?
What Are the Books of Hosea–Micah?
What Are the Books of Nahum–Malachi?

What Is the Gospel of Matthew?
What Is the Gospel of Mark?
What Is the Gospel of Luke?
What Is the Gospel of John?
What Is the Book of Acts?
What Is the Book of Romans?
What Is the Book of 1 Corinthians?
What Is the Book of 2 Corinthians?
What Is the Book of Galatians?
What Is the Book of Ephesians?
What Is the Book of Philippians?
What Are the Books of Colossians
& Philemon?
What Are the Books of 1–2 Thessalonians?
What Are the Books of 1–2 Timothy & Titus?
What Is the Book of Hebrews?
What Is the Book of James?
What Are the Books of 1–2 Peter & Jude?
What Are the Books of 1–3 John?
What Is the Book of Revelation?

What Is the Book of
REVELATION?

Michael Whitworth

ISBN 978-1-971767-20-8

Published by Start2Finish
Bend, Oregon 97702
start2finish.org

Printed in the United States of America
30 29 28 27 26   1 2 3 4 5

CONTENTS

INTRODUCTION

If someone handed you a Bible and said, "Pick the scariest book," which one would you choose?

Most people would say Revelation. And honestly? It's hard to argue with them. Within the first few chapters you've got a terrifying figure with eyes like fire and a sword coming out of his mouth. By the middle of the book there are dragons, monsters rising from the sea, and an army of locusts with human faces and scorpion tails. By the end, the earth is shaking, cities are crumbling, and the dead are standing before a throne.

No wonder people avoid this book. It sounds like a horror movie.

But here's what almost everyone gets wrong about Revelation: it wasn't written to scare you. It was written to encourage you. The very first word of the book—"revelation"—means an unveiling, a pulling back of the curtain. God isn't trying to terrify his people. He's trying to show them what's really going on behind the scenes so they can stand firm when life gets hard.

Revelation is the most misunderstood book in the Bible. It's been turned into charts, timelines, countdown clocks, and horror fiction. People have used it to predict the end of the world roughly once per generation for the last two thousand years. They've always been wrong. And they've missed the point every time.

Because Revelation isn't a calendar. It's a promise. And the promise is simple: Jesus wins. No matter how dark things get, no matter how powerful evil seems, no matter how long God's people have to wait—the Lamb is on the throne, and nothing in heaven or earth or under the earth can change that. That's what this book is about.

WHY REVELATION MATTERS

Revelation was written by a man named John to seven real churches in an area called Asia Minor—modern-day Turkey. These weren't mega-churches with big budgets and comfortable seats. They were small, scattered groups of Christians living under the shadow of the Roman Empire. Some of them were being pressured to worship the emperor. Some were being arrested. Some had already been killed for their faith.

They were tired. They were scared. And they had one overwhelming question: *Is it worth it? Is following Jesus worth everything it's costing us?*

Revelation is God's answer. And the answer is an emphatic, thundering *yes*.

But God doesn't answer with a simple pep talk. He answers with visions—vivid, bizarre, symbol-packed visions that would have made perfect sense to people who had grown up reading the Old Testament. Revelation is absolutely stuffed with images from Genesis, Exodus, Isaiah, Ezekiel, Daniel, and the Psalms. Almost every strange symbol in the book is borrowed from somewhere else in Scripture. The problem isn't that Revelation is random. The problem is that most modern readers don't recognize the references.

That's where this book comes in. We're going to walk through Revelation together, chapter by chapter, and I'm going to help you see what John's first readers would have seen: not a confusing puzzle, but a breathtaking vision of the God who reigns, the Lamb who saves, and the future that's already been decided.

WHAT YOU'RE ABOUT TO READ

Here's a roadmap of where we're headed.

Chapter 1 opens with John's vision of the risen Jesus—not the gentle shepherd of Sunday school art, but the blazing, glorious King of kings standing among his churches. It's the vision that sets the tone for everything that follows.

Chapter 2 covers the letters to the seven churches. These are real messages to real congregations, and they're surprisingly relevant to anyone who's ever struggled with apathy, compromise, fear, or lukewarm faith.

Chapter 3 takes us into the throne room of heaven, where God is worshiped by strange and magnificent creatures—and where a sealed scroll appears that no one in the universe can open. No one, that is, except a Lamb who looks like he's been slaughtered.

Chapters 4–6 walk through the seals, trumpets, and bowls—three cycles of visions that reveal the same reality from different angles: the world is full of suffering, evil is real, but God is in control and his justice is coming. We'll meet the four horsemen, the martyrs under the altar, and the 144,000 who are sealed by God.

Chapter 7 introduces the dragon and the beasts—the unholy trinity of Satan, political power, and religious deception. This is where the famous number 666 shows up, and we'll talk about what it actually means (spoiler: it's not a barcode).

Chapters 8–9 tell the story of Babylon—the seductive world system that looks like a queen but acts like a predator—and describe her sudden, permanent collapse.

Chapter 9 brings us to the climax: the wedding of the Lamb, the rider on the white horse, the binding of Satan, and the great white throne of final judgment.

Chapter 10 ends the story where the whole Bible has been heading all along—a new heaven and a new earth, a holy city descending from God, a river of life, a tree whose leaves heal the nations, and a God who finally, permanently, irreversibly comes home to live with his people.

BEFORE YOU READ

A few things to keep in mind.

The symbols are symbols. When Revelation describes a beast with seven heads and ten horns, it's not predicting a literal monster. It's using picture language—the same kind of picture language the prophets had been using for centuries—to describe realities like empires, spiritual forces, and the struggle between good and evil. If you try to read Revelation literally, you'll end up confused. If you read it the way it was designed to be read—as an unveiling told in symbols—it will make more sense than you ever expected.

The numbers mean something. Seven means completeness. Twelve means the people of God. A thousand means an enormous, full amount. 144,000 is twelve times twelve times a thousand—the complete people of God, every last one accounted for. Once you learn the language, the numbers stop being mysterious and start being beautiful.

This book is connected to everything. Revelation is the Bible's final chapter, and it ties up threads that started in Genesis. The tree of life reappears. The serpent from the garden is finally destroyed. The curse is lifted. The exile ends. If Genesis is the Bible's opening scene, Revelation is the closing credits—and it brings every storyline home.

Revelation was meant to be heard, not decoded. The first Christians didn't sit in study groups with charts and colored markers. They listened to this book read aloud in their churches, and they were moved to worship. Revelation is meant to stir your heart before it satisfies your curiosity. If you finish this book and your first reaction is wonder and worship, you've read it right. If your first reaction is to build a timeline, you might have missed the point.

THE STORY ENDS HERE

Every book of the Bible has been heading somewhere. The promises to Abraham. The rescue from Egypt. The throne of David. The prophecies of Isaiah and Ezekiel and Daniel. The life, death, and resurrection of Jesus. The mission of the early church.

All of it has been building toward what John sees in Revelation: a world made right, a people made whole, and a God who dwells with his children forever. The dragon is destroyed.

Death is dead. Every tear is wiped away. And the Lamb who was slain before the foundation of the world reigns without rival, without end, without interruption.

That's the book of Revelation. Not a horror story. A love story. The greatest one ever told—and the only one with an ending already guaranteed.

The Lamb wins. And if you belong to him, so do you.

Turn the page.

1

A VISION OF THE RISEN KING

In C. S. Lewis's *The Lion, the Witch and the Wardrobe*, four children stumble through a magic wardrobe into a frozen world called Narnia. Before long, they hear about Aslan—a great lion who is the true king of the land. They've never seen him. They've only heard stories. But even his name stirs something deep inside them. When they ask if Aslan is safe, the answer surprises them: "Safe? Who said anything about safe? 'Course he isn't safe. But he's good. He's the King, I tell you."

When the children finally meet Aslan, they discover exactly what that means. He isn't a stuffed animal or a pet you can control. He's a real lion—enormous, golden, powerful, terrifying. And yet, when he speaks, his voice is full of warmth. He's dangerous and kind at the same time. Fierce and gentle. The kind of king who makes your knees shake and your heart sing all at once.

The apostle John once knew Jesus the way the Pevensie children came to know Aslan. Not from a distance, but up close. John had walked with Jesus, eaten meals with him, listened to his teaching, and leaned against him at the last supper. He had seen Jesus heal the sick, calm storms, and raise the dead. He had also watched him die on a cross. And then, three days later, he had seen him alive again.

But that was decades ago. Now John is an old man, exiled on a small, rocky island called Patmos—punished for refusing to stop talking about Jesus. His churches are across the sea, scattered throughout cities in what we now call Turkey. And the Roman Empire is pressing down harder than ever, demanding that everyone call Caesar "Lord and God."

Then, one Sunday, everything changes. John hears a voice behind him—not a whisper, but a blast like a trumpet. And when he turns around, he sees Jesus again. But not the way he remembers him.

This time, Jesus isn't safe. But he's good. He's the King.

A VOICE LIKE A TRUMPET

John tells us exactly when it happened: he was worshiping on the Lord's day. That's Sunday—the day Christians gathered because it was the day Jesus rose from the dead. Even in exile, even alone on an island, John was worshiping.

And right in the middle of that worship, he heard a voice behind him. It was loud—like a trumpet. In the Old Testament, a trumpet was how God got people's attention. When God came down on Mount Sinai to give Moses the Ten Commandments, there was thunder, lightning, and the blast of a trumpet so loud that the people trembled. That same kind of sound now hits John's ears on Patmos.

The voice gives John a command: "Write what you see in a book and send it to the seven churches." Then it names them—Ephesus, Smyrna, Pergamum, Thyatira, Sardis, Philadelphia, and Laodicea. These were real places, real churches, real people under real pressure. And the message John is about to receive isn't just for them. The number seven in the Bible represents completeness. These seven churches stand for the whole church—including yours.

But before John writes a single word to those churches, he has to see the one who is sending the message.

THE ONE AMONG THE LAMPSTANDS

John turns toward the voice. The first thing he sees is seven golden lampstands—and standing right in the middle of them, someone who takes his breath away.

John calls him "one like a son of man." That phrase comes straight from the Old Testament book of Daniel, where a prophet sees a vision of a figure who approaches God's throne and receives an everlasting kingdom. Every Jewish reader would have recognized the reference. This is the one Daniel saw—the ruler of all nations, the one whose kingdom never ends.

But what this figure looks like is what stops you cold. John piles up image after image, each one borrowed from the Old Testament, each one revealing something about who Jesus truly is.

He's wearing a long robe with a golden sash across his chest. That's the clothing of a priest—someone who stands between God and his people. Jesus isn't watching his churches from a distance. He's serving among them.

His head and hair are white like wool, white as snow. This echoes Daniel's description of the "Ancient of Days"—God himself, seated on his throne. The white hair doesn't mean

Jesus looks old. It means he shares God's eternal wisdom and holiness. He is not just a messenger from God. He *is* God.

His eyes are like a flame of fire. Nothing is hidden from this gaze. He sees through every excuse, every pretense, every secret. He sees the truth about his churches—the good and the bad—and no darkness can hide from those eyes.

His feet are like burnished bronze, refined in a furnace. Bronze that has been through the fire is the strongest, purest metal. These are feet that crush evil. These are feet that will not be moved.

His voice is like the roar of many waters. If you've ever stood near a massive waterfall or watched waves crash during a storm, you know the sound—so loud it fills your whole body. You don't just hear it. You feel it. That's the voice of the risen Jesus.

In his right hand he holds seven stars. We'll find out in a moment that these represent the angels—or messengers—of the seven churches. Jesus holds them. They belong to him. No one can snatch them away.

From his mouth comes a sharp, double-edged sword. This isn't a weapon you swing with your hand. It's the Word of God—the truth Jesus speaks that cuts through lies, exposes sin, and conquers evil. His words don't just describe reality. They judge it and set it right.

And his face is like the sun shining at full strength. Not a gentle sunrise. Full noon. Blazing. Too bright to look at.

Put all of these images together and the message is clear: the Jesus who once washed his disciples' feet and died on a Roman cross is now revealed as the eternal King, the holy Priest, the all-seeing Judge, the invincible Warrior, the living God. He's the same person John knew—but now John sees what was always true about him.

FALLING DOWN AND GETTING UP

What happens next is exactly what you'd expect. John collapses. "When I saw him, I fell at his feet as though dead."

This is what always happens when a human being comes face to face with God's glory. Isaiah saw the Lord on his throne and cried, "I am ruined!" Ezekiel saw the glory of God and fell facedown. Daniel saw a heavenly figure and lost all his strength. Even Moses couldn't look at God's face and live. When you see the real thing—not the watered-down, safe version, but the blazing, holy, infinite reality—you don't stay standing.

But here's the part that matters most. Jesus doesn't leave John on the ground. "He laid his right hand on me, saying, 'Fear not.'" The same hand that holds the seven stars reaches down and touches a trembling old man. The same voice that roars like the ocean speaks two of the gentlest words in the Bible: *Fear not.*

And then Jesus tells John why he doesn't have to be afraid: "I am the first and the last, and the living one. I died, and behold I am alive forevermore, and I have the keys of Death and Hades." Every piece of this matters.

"I am the first and the last." In the Old Testament, God uses this exact phrase to describe himself. There is no one before him and no one after him. He is the beginning and end of everything. Jesus is claiming to be exactly that—not just a great teacher or even a great prophet, but the eternal God.

"I died, and behold I am alive forevermore." Jesus doesn't hide from his death. He walked through it. He entered the grave—and then he walked back out. Death had its shot at the Son of God, and it lost.

"I have the keys of Death and Hades." In the ancient world, whoever held the keys had the authority. Jesus holds the keys to death itself. He decides who enters and who leaves. Death is no longer an unbeatable enemy. It's a locked door, and the risen Jesus has the only key.

For John's readers, this was everything. Some of them would face prison. Some would lose their jobs, their families, and their standing in the community. Some would be killed. And Jesus says to all of them: *I have already been through the worst thing that could happen to you. I died. And I'm still here. I hold the keys. You don't need to be afraid.*

STARS AND LAMPSTANDS

Jesus ends the vision with a command and an explanation. The command: "Write what you have seen, what is now, and what will take place after this." John is to record everything—the present condition of the churches and the unfolding of God's purposes for the future. That's what the rest of Revelation will be.

Then comes the explanation. The seven stars in Jesus' right hand are the angels of the seven churches. And the seven golden lampstands are the churches themselves.

Think about what that means. In the Old Testament, a golden lampstand stood in God's temple, holding seven lamps that burned before the Lord. It represented God's people shining his light in a dark world. Now, instead of one lampstand in one temple, there are seven—because God's people are no longer one nation in one place. They're scattered across cities, meeting in homes, surrounded by a culture that worships other gods. And Jesus stands right in the middle of them.

He's not far away. He's not watching from heaven through a telescope. He's among his churches, tending their flames, holding their messengers, seeing their struggles. The churches may be small and weak. The Roman Empire may seem invincible. But the one who walks among the lampstands is the first and the last, the living one who holds the keys of death.

That's the first thing John wants you to know before anything else in Revelation unfolds. Before the seals are opened, before the trumpets sound, before the dragon appears—you need to see this. The King is alive. He is among his people. And he says, "Fear not."

WHAT THIS MEANS FOR US

First, Jesus is more glorious than you think. Most of us have a picture of Jesus in our heads—maybe gentle, maybe holding a lamb, maybe from a painting we saw at church. Those images aren't wrong, but they're incomplete. Revelation 1 shows us the full picture: a Jesus whose eyes blaze with fire, whose voice shakes the ground, and whose face outshines the sun. This is the same Jesus who held children on his lap and wept at his friend's grave. But he's also the eternal God who rules every king and conquers every enemy. The bigger your view of Jesus, the smaller your fears become.

Second, Jesus is present with his church. He doesn't send his churches a memo and wish them well. He stands among them. He holds their messengers in his hand. Whatever your church is going through—weakness, division, pressure, exhaustion—Jesus is already there. He sees everything. He knows your situation better than you do. And he hasn't let go.

Third, you don't have to be afraid of death. The one who holds the keys of Death and Hades has already walked through the worst the grave can do. He came out the other side, alive forever. Because of that, death is not the end for anyone who belongs to him. It's a door he holds open—and on the other side is life that never ends.

Fourth, Jesus speaks, and his words demand a response. The sword from his mouth is the Word of God. It doesn't just inform us—it calls us to choose. Will we listen? Will we obey? The very first blessing in Revelation belongs to those who hear and keep what's written. This book wasn't written to satisfy curiosity. It was written to change how you live.

TALKING POINTS

1. **Each detail of Jesus' appearance—his eyes, his voice, his feet, the sword from his mouth—reveals something about who he is.** Which image stands out to you most, and why?

2. **Jesus says, "Fear not."** What kinds of fears do you think John's readers were dealing with? What fears do you deal with?

3. **Jesus said that he "has the keys of Death and Hades."** What does this mean? How would that truth encourage someone facing real danger for their faith?

4. **Jesus stands "in the midst of the lampstands."** How does knowing that Christ is present with his church change the way you think about your own church?

5. Revelation begins with a blessing for those who hear and obey its message. Why is obedience—not just knowledge—so important?

The seven churches are about to hear directly from this blazing, gentle, terrifying, comforting King. He knows every one of them—their strengths, their failures, their secrets. And he has something to say to each one.

Turn the page.

2

LETTERS TO SEVEN CHURCHES

Imagine getting a report card that doesn't just list your grades—it lists everything. Not just how you did on the math test, but whether you've been kind to the kid who sits alone at lunch. Whether you actually care about what you're learning or just go through the motions. Whether you've been brave when it was hard or quiet when you should have spoken up. And imagine the teacher writing personal comments that are so specific, so accurate, that you realize they've been watching you more closely than you ever knew.

That's basically what happens in Revelation 2–3. The risen Jesus—the blazing, terrifying, gentle King from chapter 1—now sits down and dictates seven letters. One for each of the seven churches. And these aren't form letters. Each one is personal, specific, and uncomfortably honest. He knows their strengths. He knows their secrets. He praises what deserves praising. And he confronts what needs confronting.

These seven churches were real congregations in real cities scattered across western Asia Minor—modern-day Turkey. But remember, seven is the number of completeness in

Revelation. These letters aren't just for those churches. They're for every church in every age. Including yours.

THE PATTERN

Before we walk through each letter, notice the pattern. Every letter follows the same basic structure: Jesus identifies himself using an image from the vision in chapter 1. Then he says, "I know"—I know your works, your situation, your struggles. Then comes the praise, the rebuke (or both), a call to action, and finally a promise to "the one who conquers." That word "conquers" doesn't mean wins a battle with a sword. It means endures. Stays faithful. Doesn't give up or give in.

Each letter also ends with the same warning: "He who has an ear, let him hear what the Spirit says to the churches." In other words: this isn't just for them. This is for you.

EPHESUS: RIGHT ANSWERS, COLD HEART

Ephesus was the biggest and most important city on the list. It had a famous temple to the goddess Artemis—one of the wonders of the ancient world. The church there had been planted by the apostle Paul and later shepherded by Timothy and possibly John himself. These believers had a rock-solid reputation. They worked hard, endured suffering, and refused to tolerate false teachers. They tested people who claimed to be apostles and found them to be liars. Their theology was sharp. Their discipline was firm.

But Jesus saw something they couldn't see in the mirror: "You have abandoned the love you had at first." They had become so focused on being right that they forgot to be loving. They could win every argument but had lost the warmth that made their faith alive. Think of it this way: imagine someone who follows every rule in the house perfectly—makes the bed, does the dishes, finishes homework—but never hugs their parents, never laughs at dinner, never actually enjoys being part of the family. That's Ephesus. Obedient but cold.

Jesus tells them to remember, repent, and return to the things they did when their love was real. If they don't, he'll remove their lampstand—their light will go out. But for those who conquer, there's a promise that reaches all the way back to the beginning of the Bible: they will eat from the tree of life. What Adam and Eve lost in the garden, Jesus will restore.

SMYRNA: POOR BUT RICH

Smyrna was beautiful and proud—a city fiercely loyal to Rome. For Christians there, life was brutal. Because they refused to say "Caesar is Lord," they were shut out of jobs, slandered by enemies, and thrown into poverty. To them, Jesus introduces himself as "the first and the last, who died and came to life." The one who already beat death is speaking to people who might have to face it.

"I know your tribulation and your poverty," he says. Then he adds something stunning: "But you are rich." The world looked at them and saw losers. Heaven looked at them and saw treasure.

Jesus doesn't promise that the suffering will stop. He actually warns them it will get worse—some will be imprisoned. But he sets a limit: "ten days." The trial will be intense but temporary. And the command is simple and costly: "Be faithful unto death, and I will give you the crown of life."

Smyrna receives no rebuke. None. They are one of only two churches Jesus has nothing bad to say about. Sometimes the churches that look weakest to the world are the ones that shine brightest in heaven.

PERGAMUM: BRAVE BUT COMPROMISED

Pergamum was the political capital of the region, filled with temples to Zeus, to the healing god Asclepius (whose symbol was a serpent), and to the Roman emperor. Jesus calls it the place "where Satan's throne is." Living as a Christian there took real courage. One of their members, a man named Antipas, had already been killed for his faith. Jesus calls him "my faithful witness"—the same title Jesus carries himself.

So these Christians were brave. They held fast to Jesus' name under enormous pressure. But courage in one area doesn't guarantee faithfulness in every area. Some in the church had started following the teaching of the Nicolaitans—people who said it was fine to participate in pagan feasts and compromise with the culture. Their logic probably sounded reasonable: "We have to live in this city. We have to get along. What's the harm?"

Jesus' answer is blunt: repent, or I will come and fight against them with the sword of my mouth. His Word draws a line that compromise wants to blur.

To the faithful, he promises "hidden manna"—heavenly bread, the kind of provision God gave Israel in the wilderness—and a white stone with a new name. The white stone may have been an ancient symbol of acceptance or acquittal. Either way, the message is clear: God's approval matters more than the culture's.

THYATIRA: LOVING BUT GULLIBLE

Thyatira was a small city dominated by trade guilds—ancient versions of business associations. If you wanted to work, you joined a guild. If you joined a guild, you attended their feasts. And those feasts involved meat sacrificed to idols and behavior that Christians had no business being part of. The pressure to go along to get along was enormous.

The church there had a lot going for it. Jesus praises their love, faith, service, and endurance. Their recent work was even better than their earlier work—they were growing. But they had a fatal blind spot: they tolerated a woman Jesus calls "Jezebel" (a nickname drawn from one of the most wicked queens in the Old Testament). This woman was teaching that compromise with pagan culture was acceptable—maybe even sophisticated. Jesus had given her time to repent. She refused.

The lesson is hard but important: love without discernment is dangerous. Being kind doesn't mean accepting everything. Sometimes the most loving thing a church can do is say, "That teaching is wrong, and it will hurt you."

To those who resist and hold fast, Jesus promises authority over the nations and "the morning star"—a title he claims for himself. The faithful will not just share his kingdom; they will share his presence forever.

SARDIS: FAMOUS BUT DEAD

The city of Sardis sat on a steep hill and was considered nearly unconquerable. Twice in its history, enemies captured it by sneaking up a cliff while the guards slept. The city's downfall was always the same: overconfidence.

That history fits the church perfectly. Jesus' words are the bluntest of all seven letters: "You have the reputation of being alive, but you are dead." From the outside, this church probably looked impressive—programs, activities, respectability. But Jesus saw through the performance to the heart, and the heart had stopped beating. There was motion without life. Form without power. Like a phone that looks fine on the outside but has a dead battery—it can't do the one thing it was made to do.

"Wake up," Jesus says. "Strengthen what remains and is about to die." He warns them that if they don't, he will come like a thief—unexpected and unavoidable.

But even in Sardis, a few people had "not soiled their garments." They had stayed faithful when everyone around them was coasting. Jesus promises them white robes, permanent names in the book of life, and acknowledgment before the Father. Sardis teaches a sobering truth: reputation means nothing without reality. God isn't impressed by how things look.

PHILADELPHIA: SMALL BUT FAITHFUL

If Sardis was famous but dead, Philadelphia was small but alive. This church had almost nothing going for it by worldly standards. The city sat on earthquake-prone ground and had been devastated more than once. The church was weak, under pressure from hostile opponents, and had very little influence.

Jesus has nothing bad to say about them. Not one word of rebuke. Instead, he says something extraordinary: "I know that you have but little power, and yet you have kept my word and have not denied my name."

He introduces himself as the one who holds "the key of

David"—meaning he alone decides who enters his kingdom and who doesn't. And he has placed before this church "an open door, which no one is able to shut." No matter what their enemies say, no matter how many people try to lock them out, the door into God's kingdom stands wide open for them.

To the faithful, Jesus promises something that would have meant the world to people living in an earthquake zone: "I will make him a pillar in the temple of my God. Never shall he go out of it." No more shaking. No more crumbling. Permanent stability in God's presence forever.

Philadelphia proves that spiritual strength has nothing to do with size, money, or influence. A small, faithful church can display the greatness of God more powerfully than the largest building or the loudest crowd.

LAODICEA: RICH BUT BLIND

Laodicea was the wealthiest city on the list—a center of banking, famous for its black wool clothing and its medical school that produced eye salve. When an earthquake destroyed the city, Laodicea rebuilt itself without any help from Rome. They were proud, self-sufficient, and comfortable. And their church was exactly the same. "I am rich," they said. "I have prospered, and I need nothing."

Jesus' diagnosis is devastating: "You are wretched, pitiable, poor, blind, and naked." They had confused financial comfort with spiritual health. They thought everything was fine because the bank account was full. They couldn't see that their souls were starving.

Then comes the famous image. The nearby city of

Hierapolis had hot springs—useful for healing. The city of Colossae had cold, pure water—refreshing and clean. But Laodicea's water supply came through a long aqueduct and arrived lukewarm and mineral-heavy—the kind of water that makes you gag. "Because you are lukewarm," Jesus says, "I will spit you out of my mouth." They were neither hot enough to heal nor cold enough to refresh. They were useless.

But even here, Jesus' rebuke comes from love. "Those whom I love, I reprove and discipline." He tells them to buy from him gold refined by fire (real spiritual wealth), white garments (real righteousness), and eye salve (real spiritual vision). Everything the city was famous for—banking, textiles, medicine—Jesus flips on its head to show them what they actually need.

Then comes one of the most personal invitations in the Bible: "Behold, I stand at the door and knock. If anyone hears my voice and opens the door, I will come in to him and eat with him, and he with me." Even a church this far gone can open the door again. Fellowship with Jesus isn't automatic—it's a choice. And the promise to the one who conquers is staggering: "I will grant him to sit with me on my throne." The one who was sitting comfortably on earthly wealth may one day share the throne of the Lamb.

WHAT THIS MEANS FOR US

First, every church has strengths and weaknesses. No congregation gets a perfect score. Some are strong in truth but weak in love. Some are loving but gullible. Some are famous but empty. The seven letters remind us that Jesus sees it all—the good, the bad, and the things we think we've hidden.

Second, comfort and Christ are not the same thing. Laodicea had everything the world admires and nothing Jesus valued. Smyrna had nothing the world admires and everything Jesus valued. Wealth, reputation, and influence can actually blind us to our real spiritual condition.

Third, endurance is the mark of a true Christian. Over and over, the promises go to "the one who conquers." That doesn't mean the one who never struggles. It means the one who never quits. Faithfulness isn't about being perfect. It's about holding on to Jesus when everything else tries to pull you away.

Fourth, Jesus is still speaking to his churches. These letters weren't just for the first century. Every warning, every promise, every "I know" still applies. Jesus still walks among the lampstands. He still sees. He still calls. And he still knocks.

TALKING POINTS

1. Which of the seven churches sounds most like a church you've experienced? Why?

2. **Ephesus was right about doctrine but had lost its love.** How can someone be "correct" but still miss the point of faith?

3. **Smyrna and Philadelphia received no rebuke—and both were small and suffering.** What does that tell us about how God measures success?

4. What does compromise look like for a Christian your age? Where are the pressure points to "go along to get along"?

5. **Jesus told Laodicea, "You say you are rich, but you are actually poor."** How can comfort and wealth trick us into thinking we don't need God?

The King has spoken to his churches. He has seen them clearly—their love and their failures, their courage and their compromise. Now the scene shifts. John is about to be pulled through an open door into heaven itself, where he will see the throne that rules the universe and the Lamb who alone can open the scroll of history.

Turn the page.

3

THE THRONE ROOM AND THE LAMB

In Madeleine L'Engle's *A Wrinkle in Time*, there's a moment that changes how Meg sees everything. She and her companions have traveled across the universe searching for her missing father, and they're frightened—a great darkness called The Black Thing is spreading across the galaxies, swallowing planets in shadow. From where Meg stands, evil looks unstoppable.

Then Mrs. Whatsit takes the children to a mountaintop and shows them something they couldn't see from the ground: the stars themselves are fighting back. Light is pushing against the darkness. The battle is real, but it's not hopeless—because forces far greater than Meg ever imagined are already at work. She just couldn't see them until someone brought her high enough to look.

Revelation 4 is John's mountaintop moment. For three chapters he's been on the ground with the seven churches—watching them struggle under Rome's shadow, delivering urgent messages to tired, pressured Christians. From street level, the empire looks unstoppable. Then a door opens in heaven, a voice says "Come up here," and John is lifted above the fog of earthly chaos into the one place where everything finally makes sense: the throne room of God. What he sees there isn't panic. It's worship. The throne isn't empty. It's blazing with glory. And the future of the world isn't in the emperor's hands—it's in a sealed scroll, and only one figure in the universe can open it.

Before the seals break. Before the horsemen ride. Before a single trumpet sounds. God wants you to see who's really in charge.

A DOOR STANDING OPEN

"After this I looked, and behold, a door standing open in heaven!" That's how chapter 4 begins. The same trumpet-like voice from chapter 1 calls out to John: "Come up here, and I will show you what must take place after this." Immediately, John is "in the Spirit"—caught up in a prophetic vision, like Ezekiel and Isaiah before him. His physical surroundings on Patmos fade away. What opens before him is the hidden reality behind everything that happens on earth.

And the very first thing he sees is a throne. Not an empty throne. Not a crumbling throne. A throne with someone sitting on it—blazing with light like precious stones, surrounded by flashes of lightning, rumbles of thunder, and seven torches of fire. This is the command center of the universe. Everything that follows in Revelation—every seal, every trumpet, every judgment—flows from this throne. Before you see the chaos of earth, God wants you to see the order of heaven.

Why does this matter? Because the churches John is writing to lived under the shadow of another throne—Rome's.

The emperor Domitian demanded to be called "Our Lord and God." His throne projected power through fear, military force, and propaganda. And from the street level, it looked unbeatable. But John has just been shown the real throne. And it makes Rome's look like a folding chair.

WHAT JOHN SEES AROUND THE THRONE

The scene John describes is overwhelming. He piles up images the way a painter layers color—not to give a photograph of heaven, but to communicate what it feels like to stand in the presence of the living God.

The one on the throne gleams like jasper and carnelian—brilliant, radiant stones that shimmer with purity and majesty. Around the throne stretches an emerald rainbow. In the Old Testament, the rainbow was the sign of God's promise to Noah that he would never again destroy the earth with a flood. Here, it wraps around the very seat of divine power, reminding us that the God who judges is also the God who keeps his promises. His power is bound by his mercy.

In front of the throne burns seven torches of fire, which John identifies as the seven spirits of God—a symbolic picture of the Holy Spirit in all his fullness. There is also a sea of glass, crystal clear and perfectly still. In the ancient world, the sea represented chaos, danger, and evil. But before God's throne, the sea is calm. Frozen. Subdued. Whatever chaos rages on earth, it is already conquered in heaven.

Around the throne sit twenty-four elders on twenty-four thrones. They wear white robes and golden crowns. Most scholars believe they represent the complete people of God—

twelve for the tribes of Israel, twelve for the apostles. Old Testament and New Testament. The entire family of faith, gathered around the one who made them and saved them.

And closest to the throne are four living creatures—strange, magnificent beings covered in eyes, each with a different face: a lion, an ox, a human, and an eagle. These echo the visions of the prophet Ezekiel, where similar creatures surrounded God's glory. They seem to represent all of creation—wild animals, domesticated animals, humanity, and birds of the air—everything God made, gathered around him in worship. They are covered in eyes because nothing in all creation escapes their awareness of God's glory.

And what do these creatures do? Day and night, without stopping, they cry out: "Holy, holy, holy, is the Lord God Almighty, who was and is and is to come!"

Every time they say it, the twenty-four elders fall down, lay their crowns at God's feet, and sing: "Worthy are you, our Lord and God, to receive glory and honor and power, for you created all things, and by your will they existed and were created."

Think about what's happening here. The emperor Domitian demanded that people call him "Our Lord and God." But in heaven, those words belong to someone else entirely. The elders aren't singing to Caesar. They're singing to the Creator. And every time they do, it's an act of defiance against every throne on earth that claims to be ultimate.

Worship isn't just something nice Christians do on Sunday. In Revelation, worship is resistance. It's how God's people declare who really rules.

THE SCROLL NO ONE CAN OPEN

Then John notices something in the right hand of the one on the throne: a scroll, written on both sides and sealed with seven seals. This scroll represents God's plan—his purpose for history, for justice, for setting everything right. It contains the answer to every prayer the suffering church has ever prayed: *How long, Lord? When will you act? When will evil be defeated and your promises be kept?*

A mighty angel calls out with a loud voice: "Who is worthy to open the scroll and break its seals?"

Silence. No one in heaven. No one on earth. No one under the earth. Not a single angel, not a single human being, not a single creature in the entire universe steps forward.

And John starts to weep. If nobody can open the scroll, then God's plan stays locked. Evil goes unchallenged. Justice never comes. The martyrs' blood cries out and no one answers. The prayers of the suffering pile up with no resolution. Everything the churches are enduring—the poverty, the persecution, the pressure—means nothing if the scroll stays sealed.

John weeps because the future itself seems stuck.

THE LION WHO IS A LAMB

Then one of the elders speaks: "Stop weeping. Look—the Lion of the tribe of Judah, the Root of David, has conquered. He can open the scroll and its seven seals."

The Lion of Judah. That title goes all the way back to Genesis, where the patriarch Jacob blessed his son Judah and compared him to a lion—fierce, royal, unconquerable. The Root of David points to the promised king from David's line who would reign forever. When John hears these words, he expects to turn around and see a warrior. A conqueror. A king with a crown and a sword, ready to rip open the scroll by sheer force.

But when John turns to look, he doesn't see a lion.

He sees a Lamb. Standing as though it had been slain.

This is one of the most important moments in the entire Bible. John hears "Lion" but sees "Lamb." The two images crash into each other and fuse into one. The way this king conquers is not through violence, military power, or political domination. He conquers through sacrifice. The cross—not the sword—is heaven's definition of victory.

The Lamb has seven horns, symbolizing perfect power. He has seven eyes, representing the fullness of the Spirit, sent out into all the earth. This isn't a weak, helpless animal. This is the most powerful being in the universe. But his power doesn't look like Rome's power. His power looks like love poured out, like blood shed for others, like a life given so that others might live.

The Lamb steps forward and takes the scroll from the right hand of the one on the throne.

And heaven explodes.

HEAVEN'S SONG

The four living creatures and the twenty-four elders fall down before the Lamb. They hold golden bowls filled with incense, which John tells us are "the prayers of the saints." Every prayer those persecuted churches had ever whispered—every "How long?" every "Help us," every "Don't forget us"—those prayers are right here, rising like perfume before the throne of God.

They haven't been ignored. They haven't been lost. They are part of the worship of heaven.

And then the elders sing a new song: "Worthy are you to take the scroll and to open its seals, for you were slain, and by your blood you ransomed people for God from every tribe and language and people and nation, and you have made them a kingdom and priests to our God, and they shall reign on the earth."

Notice what makes Jesus worthy. It's not raw power. It's not military conquest. It's his death. He was slain, and through his sacrifice he purchased people from every corner of the earth—not by force, but by love. He didn't build an empire through domination. He built a kingdom through redemption.

And look who he ransomed: every tribe, language, people, and nation. In a world where Rome unified people through conquest and fear, the Lamb unifies them through blood freely given. No ethnicity excluded. No language too obscure. No nation too far away. The Lamb's kingdom is bigger than Rome ever dreamed of being—and it was built without a single act of violence.

Then the circle of worship widens. Thousands upon thousands of angels join in—"myriads of myriads and thousands of thousands"—singing with a loud voice: "Worthy is the Lamb who was slain, to receive power and wealth and wisdom and might and honor and glory and blessing!" Every possible form of praise and authority, given to the slaughtered Lamb. In Rome, these words belonged to the emperor. In heaven, they belong to Jesus.

And then, in the final moment, every creature in existence joins the chorus—everything in heaven and on earth and under the earth and in the sea: "To him who sits on the throne and to the Lamb be blessing and honor and glory and might forever and ever!" The four living creatures say, "Amen!" The elders fall down and worship.

The scene is over. And nothing will ever look the same again.

WHAT THIS MEANS FOR US

First, the throne comes before the trouble. Revelation doesn't start with disasters and dragons. It starts with God on his throne. That order matters. Before you face anything frightening in this book—or in life—you need to know who's in charge. The answer isn't the government, the economy, or whatever crisis is dominating the news. The answer is the one on the throne, surrounded by a rainbow of mercy, worshiped by all creation. If you get this scene right, everything that follows makes sense.

Second, the Lamb redefines power. We live in a world that admires strength, size, wealth, and control. The Lamb flips all of that upside down. The most powerful being in the universe conquered not by killing but by dying. Not by taking but by giving. If you want to know what real strength looks like, don't look at the biggest army or the richest billionaire. Look at the Lamb who was slain and is standing alive. That's what power looks like in God's kingdom.

Third, your prayers matter more than you know. Those golden bowls of incense are the prayers of ordinary Christians—people like John's churches, people like you. They didn't disappear into silence. They rose to heaven's throne and became part of the worship that shakes the universe. When you pray and it feels like nothing is happening, remember the bowls. God keeps every word.

Fourth, worship is an act of allegiance. Every time the

elders cast their crowns and cry "Worthy!"—they're choosing. They're declaring that God alone deserves their loyalty. In a world full of things competing for your worship—popularity, money, status, comfort—singing to the Lamb is how you say, "I belong to a different kingdom." Worship isn't escape from the real world. It's how you see the real world clearly.

TALKING POINTS

1. **Revelation shows the throne room *before* showing the troubles of earth.** Why do you think it does so? How does that change how you read the rest of the book?

2. **John hears "Lion" but sees "Lamb."** What does that tell us about how God defines power and victory?

3. **The elders cast their crowns before the throne.** What "crowns" do people your age tend to hold onto—achievements, popularity, reputation? What would it look like to lay those down?

4. **The prayers of the saints fill golden bowls in heaven.** How does that change the way you think about prayer—especially when it feels like God isn't listening?

5. **The emperor Domitian demanded to be called "Our Lord and God." The elders use those same words for the Creator.** How is worship an act of resistance against the things that compete for our loyalty today?

The throne is established. The Lamb has taken the scroll. Heaven is singing. Now it's time to see what happens when the seals begin to break—and the Lamb starts to reveal what God's plan for history actually looks like.

Turn the page.

4

THE FOUR HORSEMEN AND THE PEOPLE WHO STAND

In *The Hunger Games*, Katniss Everdeen is thrown into an arena she didn't choose, facing dangers she can't control. Powerful people in the Capitol designed the whole thing. They send fire, flood, and deadly creatures whenever they want. From inside the arena, everything looks random—chaotic, terrifying, hopeless. But from the control room, someone is watching every move. Nothing happens by accident.

Revelation 6–7 puts the church inside an arena. Not a fictional one, but the real world—with its wars, famines, injustice, and death. The first-century Christians reading this letter knew the arena well. Rome was powerful. Christians were hunted. The world felt out of control.

But John has already shown his readers the control room. Chapters 4–5 revealed the throne of God and the Lamb who holds the scroll. Now the Lamb begins to open that scroll, one seal at a time. And what comes out isn't pretty. Four horsemen ride across the earth, bringing conquest, violence, scarcity, and death. Martyrs cry out from under an altar. The sky goes dark and the mountains shake.

It's terrifying. But here's the difference between this story and *The Hunger Games*: the one in the control room isn't cruel. He's the slaughtered Lamb who conquered by love. And the most important question in these chapters isn't "What's coming next?" It's the question shouted at the end of chapter 6: "Who can stand?"

Chapter 7 answers it.

THE LAMB OPENS THE SEALS

Remember the scroll from chapter 5—the one sealed with seven seals that no one in the universe could open? The Lamb was the only one found worthy. Now he begins breaking those seals. And with each one, something is released into the world.

It's important to understand what's happening here. These seals aren't a calendar of events counting down to the end of the world. They're more like a curtain being pulled back on reality—showing the kinds of things the church will face throughout its entire history, from the first century to now. The Lamb isn't causing evil. He's revealing what's already at work in a broken world, and he's showing that none of it is outside his authority.

Each of the first four seals is introduced by one of the four living creatures from the throne room. With a voice like thunder, each one says, "Come!" And a horse and rider appear.

THE FOUR HORSEMEN

The white horse. The first rider carries a bow and wears a crown. He rides out "conquering, and to conquer." This horse represents the human hunger for domination—the drive to conquer, control, and build empires. Every century has its version. Babylon, Persia, Rome, and every empire since. The lust for power never stops riding.

The red horse. The second rider carries a great sword and is given the power to "take peace from the earth." This is war and violence—not one specific war, but the bloodshed that stains every generation of human history. Wherever the desire to conquer goes, violence follows.

The black horse. The third rider holds a pair of scales. A voice calls out: "A quart of wheat for a denarius"—a full day's wages for barely enough food to survive—"but do not harm the oil and wine." This is economic injustice. The poor go hungry while the luxuries of the wealthy stay untouched. The scales are rigged. The system is broken.

The pale horse. The fourth rider is named Death, and Hades follows close behind him. He is given authority over a fourth of the earth, to kill by sword, famine, plague, and wild beasts. This is death in its most sweeping form—the kind that touches everyone, believer and unbeliever alike. It echoes the prophet Ezekiel's description of God's four deadly judgments.

Together, the four horsemen paint a picture of the world as it has always been: power-hungry, violent, unjust, and deadly. John's readers weren't hearing a prediction about some distant future. They were hearing a description of the world they already lived in. And so are we.

But notice something crucial. The horsemen don't ride on their own authority. Each one is released by the Lamb. Each one is summoned by the living creatures around the throne. The fourth rider is given authority over only a fourth of the earth—his power has limits. The chaos of the world is real, but it is not ultimate. The Lamb still holds the scroll. The throne still stands.

THE CRY UNDER THE ALTAR

When the Lamb opens the fifth seal, the scene shifts. John is no longer looking at the earth. He's looking at an altar in heaven, and underneath it he sees the souls of people who had been killed for their faithfulness to God and his word.

These are the martyrs—believers who held on to their testimony and paid for it with their lives. And they cry out: "How long, O Lord, holy and true, until you judge and avenge our blood on those who dwell on the earth?"

This isn't a cry for personal revenge. It's a cry for justice. It's the same prayer God's people have prayed for centuries: *How long will evil go unpunished? How long will the wicked win? When will you set things right?*

God's answer is tender but honest. Each martyr is given a white robe—a sign of honor, purity, and victory. And they are told to "rest a little longer," because more believers will yet join them in suffering before the end comes.

That might sound like a hard answer. But it's actually a promise. God hasn't forgotten them. Their blood hasn't been wasted. Their prayers haven't disappeared. Justice is coming—but on heaven's schedule, not earth's. And in the meantime, their voices join the worship of heaven, and their sacrifice becomes the seed of the church's endurance for generations to come.

If you've ever prayed and felt like God wasn't listening— this scene is for you. Revelation says your prayers rise to the very throne of God. They matter. They are heard. And they will be answered.

THE EARTH SHAKES

The sixth seal is the most dramatic yet. When the Lamb breaks it, creation itself convulses. A massive earthquake. The sun turns black. The moon turns red as blood. Stars fall from the sky. The sky rolls up like a scroll. Mountains and islands are torn from their places.

These images come straight from the Old Testament prophets—Isaiah, Ezekiel, and Joel—and they describe the collapse of human power under the weight of God's judgment. Kings, generals, the rich, the powerful, and the enslaved all hide in caves and cry out for the mountains to fall on them: "Hide us from the face of him who sits on the throne, and from the wrath of the Lamb!"

Even the mightiest people on earth—the ones who seemed untouchable—are terrified. Every throne that isn't God's throne is shaking.

And then comes the question that echoes through the chaos: "Who can stand?"

It's the most important question in these two chapters. If God's judgment shakes everything—if no king, no general, no fortune can protect you—then who survives? Who makes it through?

John doesn't answer right away. Instead, he pauses. And what comes next is one of the most comforting scenes in the entire Bible.

SEALED BY GOD

Before the seventh seal is opened, four angels stand at the four corners of the earth, holding back the winds of destruction. A fifth angel rises from the east, carrying the seal of the living God. He calls out with a loud voice: "Do not harm the earth or the sea or the trees, until we have sealed the servants of our God on their foreheads."

In the ancient world, a seal meant three things: ownership, protection, and identity. When a king stamped his seal on something, it meant, "This belongs to me. Don't touch it." That's what God is doing here. Before the storm comes, he marks his people. They are his. They are known. They are kept.

The seal doesn't mean Christians won't suffer. The horsemen have already ridden. The martyrs have already died. But the seal means that no suffering—not war, not famine, not death itself—can separate God's people from his love or erase their names from his book.

John hears the number of those sealed: 144,000—twelve thousand from each of the twelve tribes of Israel. But this number isn't meant to be taken as a literal headcount. It's symbolic. Twelve (the number of God's people) times twelve, times a thousand (the number of vastness and completeness). It means *all* of God's people. Every single one. Not one is missing. Not one is forgotten.

THE CROWD NO ONE CAN COUNT

Then John turns to look—and what he sees is staggering. "After this I looked, and behold, a great multitude that no one could number, from every nation, from all tribes and peoples and languages, standing before the throne and before the Lamb, clothed in white robes, with palm branches in their hands."

He heard a number—144,000. But he sees a crowd so enormous it can't be counted. This is the same group, seen from two angles. The 144,000 is the church on earth—counted, sealed, and known by God in the middle of its struggles. The great multitude is the church in glory—triumphant, celebrating, and finally home.

They come from every nation. Every tribe. Every language. Every people group on earth. The Lamb's kingdom isn't limited to one country, one culture, or one century. It's the most diverse gathering in the history of the universe, united not by politics or ethnicity but by the blood of the Lamb.

They wave palm branches—an ancient symbol of victory and celebration—and they shout with one voice: "Salvation belongs to our God who sits on the throne, and to the Lamb!"

That's their answer to the question "Who can stand?" They can. Not because they were strong enough or smart enough or lucky enough. But because salvation belongs to God and to the Lamb. They stand because he holds them.

One of the elders turns to John and asks, "Who are these people in white robes, and where did they come from?" John says, "Sir, you know." The elder answers: "These are the ones coming out of the great tribulation. They have washed their robes and made them white in the blood of the Lamb."

The "great tribulation" here doesn't mean a specific future event. It means the whole struggle—the full weight of suffering that God's people face throughout history. These are the ones who made it through. Not around it, not above it—through it.

And the thing that made them clean wasn't their own strength. It was the Lamb's blood. A paradox: robes washed white in blood. Purity through sacrifice. Victory through the cross.

The vision ends with one of the most beautiful promises in all of Scripture: "They shall hunger no more, neither thirst anymore; the sun shall not strike them, nor any scorching heat. For the Lamb in the midst of the throne will be their shepherd, and he will guide them to springs of living water, and God will wipe away every tear from their eyes."

Every tear. Not just the big ones. Every single tear that suffering, injustice, loss, and death ever caused—God himself will wipe them away. The horsemen ride for a while. But the Lamb shepherds forever.

WHAT THIS MEANS FOR US

First, the world's chaos is real, but it isn't ultimate. The horsemen are terrifying. War, injustice, and death are not imaginary. But they ride within limits set by the Lamb. They do not have the final word. When the news feels overwhelming, Revelation says: the throne still stands.

Second, lament is an act of faith, not failure. The martyrs cry "How long?"—and God doesn't rebuke them for it. He honors them with white robes. When you're hurting and you bring that pain honestly to God, you're not doubting him. You're trusting him enough to tell him the truth.

Third, God's seal doesn't prevent suffering—it preserves through it. Being a Christian doesn't mean life gets easy. It means you belong to someone whose grip is stronger than anything the world can throw at you. The seal says: "You are mine, and nothing changes that."

Fourth, the ending is already written. The great multitude is standing. The robes are white. The tears are wiped away. The Lamb is shepherding his people to living water. Whatever chapter of the story you're living in right now—the last chapter has already been seen. And it's good.

TALKING POINTS

1. **The four horsemen represent things that happen in every century—not just the future.** How does that change the way you read this passage?

2. **The martyrs ask, "How long?"** Have you ever felt that way when praying? What does it mean that God honored their question with a white robe instead of a rebuke?

3. What does it mean to be "sealed" by God? How is that different from being promised an easy life?

4. **The great multitude comes from "every nation, tribe, people, and language."** Why is that important for understanding the kind of kingdom Jesus is building?

5. **The chapter ends with God wiping away every tear.** What tears do you think the first-century Christians most needed wiped away? What about you?

The horsemen have ridden. The martyrs have cried out. The redeemed have been sealed and the great multitude has been seen. But the seventh seal still hasn't been opened. When it is, something unexpected happens—not a crash of thunder, but silence. And from that silence, a new wave of judgment begins.

Turn the page.

5

TRUMPETS, A SCROLL, AND TWO WITNESSES

In the movie *Inception*, there's a scene where a city starts folding in on itself. Streets bend upward, buildings crack and tilt, and the whole world warps as gravity loses its grip. The characters inside the dream know something is wrong—the environment is responding to forces they can't see. What looks like random destruction is actually being caused by someone in control, someone shaping the dream from the outside.

Revelation 8–11 feels a lot like that. Mountains burn and fall into the sea. Rivers turn bitter. The sky goes dark. Locusts swarm out of a smoking pit. Armies of destruction ride across the earth. From the ground level, it looks like the world is coming apart. But John has already shown us the throne room. He's already revealed who holds the scroll. And now, as the seventh seal is opened and seven trumpets begin to sound, we learn something important: these judgments aren't random. They aren't chaos. They are controlled, measured, and purposeful. And they start with something nobody expects.

Silence.

SILENCE IN HEAVEN

When the Lamb opens the seventh seal, you'd expect a crash of thunder or a blast of worship. Instead: "There was silence in heaven for about half an hour." In a book crammed with sound—trumpets, voices, songs, thunder—this silence is shocking. Heaven holds its breath. Why?

Because an angel approaches the golden altar with a censer full of incense, and mixed with that incense are the prayers of the saints. Every cry of "How long?" from the martyrs under the altar. Every whispered prayer from a persecuted Christian in a Roman prison. Every honest plea for justice. They rise together before the throne of God like a cloud of fragrant smoke.

Then the angel takes the censer, fills it with fire from the altar, and hurls it to the earth. Thunder, lightning, and an earthquake follow.

Here's what that means: the judgments that are about to unfold are not acts of random anger. They are God's response to the prayers of his people. The saints prayed. Heaven listened. And now heaven answers. In Revelation, prayer doesn't just comfort the one who prays—it moves history.

THE FIRST FOUR TRUMPETS

Seven angels stand ready, each holding a trumpet. In the Bible, trumpets aren't musical instruments for entertainment. They announce God's presence, warn of danger, and call people to attention. Think of the trumpets at the battle of Jericho, or the trumpet blast at Mount Sinai. When God's trumpet sounds, it means something is happening that you cannot ignore.

The first four trumpets strike the natural world—the same creation that sang "Holy, holy, holy" in chapter 4 now groans under the weight of human rebellion.

The **first trumpet** brings hail and fire mixed with blood. A third of the earth, a third of the trees, and all the green grass are scorched. The **second trumpet** sends something like a blazing mountain crashing into the sea. A third of the sea turns to blood, a third of the sea creatures die, and a third of the ships are destroyed. The **third trumpet** drops a burning star called Wormwood—meaning "bitterness"—into the rivers and springs. A third of the fresh water turns poisonous, and many people die. The **fourth trumpet** strikes the sky itself: a third of the sun, moon, and stars go dark.

These images echo the plagues God sent on Egypt when Pharaoh refused to let his people go—blood, darkness, destruction. John's readers would have caught the parallel immediately. Just as Egypt oppressed God's people and suffered for it, the world that persecutes God's church will feel the consequences.

But notice the word that keeps repeating: **a third**. Not all. Not most. A third. These judgments are severe, but they are restrained. God isn't trying to annihilate—he's trying to wake people up. The trumpets are warnings, not final sentences. They're alarm bells, not death knells.

Then an eagle flies across the sky and cries: "Woe, woe, woe to those who dwell on the earth, because of the remaining blasts of the three trumpets!" If the first four were bad, what comes next is worse. The last three trumpets shift from the natural world to the spiritual one.

LOCUSTS FROM THE PIT

The fifth trumpet opens the abyss—a bottomless pit—and thick smoke billows out like smoke from a furnace, darkening the sun and the air. Out of the smoke pour locusts. But these aren't ordinary bugs eating crops. These are nightmare creatures: shaped like warhorses, with human faces, lion's teeth, iron breastplates, and scorpion tails that sting. Their wings sound like an army of chariots charging into battle. Their king is called Abaddon—"the Destroyer."

What is this?

John is using terrifying images to describe something real: the spiritual destruction that comes from living apart from God. These locusts represent the misery, despair, and inner torment that evil brings into human life. They aren't sent to harm those who are sealed by God—only those who have refused him. The suffering they cause is so intense that people "seek death and do not find it." They want escape, but there is none.

Yet even this horror has limits. The locusts torment for five months—a normal locust season—meaning their power is temporary, not eternal. The Destroyer may rage, but he operates on a leash held by the Lamb. Evil in Revelation is never free. It is always permitted, always limited, and always under the authority of the one on the throne.

ARMIES OF DESTRUCTION

The sixth trumpet releases four angels bound at the Euphrates River. For John's readers, the Euphrates was the edge of the known world—the boundary where Roman civilization ended and terrifying enemies began. To mention the Euphrates was to invoke the deepest fears of invasion and chaos.

An army of two hundred million riders sweeps across the earth, breathing fire, smoke, and sulfur. A third of humanity is killed. This isn't a description of one specific war. It's a portrait of what war has always done throughout human history—the devastation that human violence unleashes when sin runs unchecked.

And then comes one of the saddest verses in Revelation: "The rest of mankind, who were not killed by these plagues, did not repent of the works of their hands nor give up worshiping demons and idols of gold and silver and bronze and stone and wood, which cannot see or hear or walk, nor did they repent of their murders or their sorceries or their sexual immorality or their thefts."

Six trumpets have sounded. Creation has shaken. Darkness has fallen. Armies have ridden. And still—people refuse to turn back to God. They cling to idols that can't see, hear, or walk. That's the tragedy at the heart of these chapters. The trumpets are mercy dressed as judgment—God shaking the world to get its attention. But shaking alone doesn't change hearts. Only the Spirit can do that.

A SCROLL TO EAT

Before the seventh trumpet sounds, there's a pause—just like the pause between the sixth and seventh seals. And in this pause, John sees two visions that shift the focus from judgment back to the church.

First, a mighty angel descends from heaven holding a small open scroll. He plants one foot on the sea and one on the land—a picture of authority over the entire world—and tells John to take the scroll and eat it. "It will be sweet as honey in your mouth," the angel says, "but it will make your stomach bitter."

John eats it. It's sweet. Then it's bitter. And the angel tells him: "You must prophesy again about many peoples and nations and languages and kings."

What does this mean? The scroll is God's word—the message John must proclaim. It's sweet because the gospel is good news: God saves, the Lamb reigns, and the kingdom will come. But it's bitter because proclaiming that truth will bring suffering. It always has. The gospel comforts the afflicted, but it also confronts the powerful. And the world doesn't take kindly to being confronted.

Before the church can speak for God, it must first swallow his word—all of it. The sweet parts and the bitter parts. The promises and the warnings.

THE MEASURED TEMPLE AND THE TWO WITNESSES

Next, John is given a measuring rod and told to measure the temple of God and those who worship in it. But he's told not to measure the outer court—"it has been given to the nations, and they will trample the holy city for forty-two months."

The "temple" here isn't a building. It's a symbol for the church—God's people. To measure something in the Bible means to claim it, protect it, and mark its boundaries. God is saying: "My people belong to me. They are measured. They are known. They are secure." But the outer court—the church's visible, physical existence in the world—will be trampled. Christians will suffer. Their bodies and reputations may be crushed.

But their souls are measured by God, and no enemy can unmeasure what he has marked.

Then come the two witnesses. They prophesy for 1,260 days (the same as forty-two months), clothed in sackcloth—a sign of mourning and urgent preaching. They have the power of Moses (turning water to blood, striking the earth with plagues) and Elijah (shutting the sky so it doesn't rain, calling down fire). They represent the witnessing church throughout history—God's people faithfully proclaiming his word in a hostile world.

When their testimony is finished, a beast rises from the abyss and kills them. Their bodies lie in the street of "the great city"—symbolically called Sodom and Egypt, representing the world in its rebellion against God. The world celebrates. People send gifts to each other, thrilled that the annoying voices of truth have finally been silenced.

But after three and a half days, breath from God enters them. They stand up. Their enemies watch in terror. A voice from heaven says, "Come up here," and they ascend in a cloud.

The pattern is unmistakable. It's the pattern of Jesus himself: faithful witness, suffering, death, and resurrection. The church follows the Lamb's path. The world may silence God's witnesses for a moment, but it cannot keep them down. Death doesn't win. Vindication always comes.

THE SEVENTH TRUMPET

Finally, the seventh angel sounds his trumpet. And instead of another disaster, heaven erupts in song: "The kingdom of the world has become the kingdom of our Lord and of his Christ, and he shall reign forever and ever."

The twenty-four elders fall on their faces and worship: "We give thanks to you, Lord God Almighty, who is and who was, for you have taken your great power and begun to reign."

This is what everything has been building toward. Not destruction for its own sake. Not chaos without purpose. But this: the kingdoms of the world—every empire, every throne, every power that ever demanded worship—all of them will bow. They will become what they were always meant to be: part of the kingdom of the Lamb.

The temple in heaven opens, and the ark of the covenant becomes visible—the sign of God's faithfulness to every promise he ever made. Lightning, thunder, earthquake, and hail follow. The promise made to Abraham, fulfilled in Christ, and carried by the church has reached its destination.

The trumpets have sounded. The warnings have been given. The witnesses have testified. And the kingdom belongs to the Lamb.

WHAT THIS MEANS FOR US

First, your prayers are more powerful than you know. The judgments of the trumpets begin with the prayers of the saints rising before God's throne. When you pray for justice, for help, for the world to change—those prayers don't bounce off the ceiling. They rise like incense into the control room of the universe.

Second, God's warnings are acts of mercy. The trumpets aren't tantrums. They're alarm bells. Every shaking of the world is an invitation to wake up and turn back to God before it's too late. A third—not all—is affected, because God is still holding the door open for repentance.

Third, the church's job is to speak the truth, not to win popularity. The scroll is sweet and bitter. The two witnesses are killed for their testimony. Following the Lamb means proclaiming his word even when the world doesn't want to hear it. But vindication always follows faithfulness—always.

Fourth, the kingdom will come. The seventh trumpet doesn't announce another disaster. It announces victory. Every power that stands against God will fall. Every prayer will be answered. Every promise will be kept. The kingdom of the world will become the kingdom of our Lord and of his Christ. That's not a wish. It's a certainty.

TALKING POINTS

1. **The trumpets begin with the prayers of the saints.** How does knowing that prayer "moves history" change the way you think about praying?

2. **The trumpets affect "a third" of the earth, sea, rivers, and sky—not all.** What does that restraint tell us about what God is doing through these judgments?

3. **Despite six trumpets of warning, people in chapter 9 refuse to repent.** Why do you think suffering alone doesn't automatically change hearts?

4. **The scroll is sweet in John's mouth but bitter in his stomach.** What are the "sweet" and "bitter" parts of following Jesus?

5. **The two witnesses are killed but then raised to life.** How does their story follow the same pattern as Jesus' life? What does that mean for the church today?

The trumpets have sounded and the kingdom has been declared. But the story isn't over. Behind the world's empires and persecutions stands an ancient enemy—a dragon who has been waging war since the beginning. John is about to pull back the curtain on the deepest conflict in the universe.

Turn the page.

6

THE DRAGON AND THE BEASTS

In *Star Wars*, there's a moment in *The Empire Strikes Back* when Darth Vader reveals the truth to Luke Skywalker: the dark power Luke has been fighting isn't some distant, impersonal evil. It's personal. It has a name. It has a strategy. And it's been hunting him since the day he was born.

Revelation 12–13 is the moment John pulls back the curtain on the real enemy. Up to this point, the churches have been dealing with visible threats—Rome, persecution, false teachers, social pressure. Now John shows them what's actually behind all of it. Not just a corrupt government. Not just bad leaders. But a dragon—an ancient, intelligent, furious enemy who has been waging war against God's people since the very beginning of the story.

And this dragon doesn't work alone. He raises up two beasts—one from the sea and one from the earth—who serve as his agents in the world. Together, the three form a twisted imitation of God: a counterfeit Father, a counterfeit Christ, and a counterfeit Spirit. They're powerful. They're convincing. And they demand worship.

But here's what John's readers needed to know more than anything: the dragon has already lost.

THE WOMAN AND THE DRAGON

The vision opens with two enormous signs in heaven. The first is a woman clothed with the sun, the moon under her feet, and a crown of twelve stars on her head. She's pregnant, crying out in the pain of childbirth.

This woman isn't one person. She represents the people of God—first Israel, through whom the Messiah was promised, and then the church, through whom his kingdom continues. The twelve stars recall the twelve tribes of Israel, the twelve apostles, and the complete family of faith across all of history.

The second sign is a great red dragon with seven heads, ten horns, and seven crowns. John doesn't leave us guessing who this is. A few verses later he spells it out: "that ancient serpent, who is called the devil and Satan, the deceiver of the whole world." The seven heads represent cunning intelligence. The ten horns represent enormous power. The crowns represent stolen authority. His tail sweeps a third of the stars from the sky—a picture of his destructive influence over the angels who fell with him.

The dragon crouches in front of the woman, waiting to devour her child the moment he's born. This is the oldest conflict in the Bible—the one God promised in Genesis 3:15, when he told the serpent that the woman's offspring would crush his head. From Pharaoh trying to kill the baby Moses, to Herod trying to kill the baby Jesus, the dragon has always tried to destroy the child before he can fulfill his mission.

But in one breathtaking sentence, the child is born, caught up to God, and seated on his throne. The life, death, resurrection, and ascension of Jesus are compressed into a single line—because from heaven's perspective, the dragon never had a chance. His plan to destroy the Messiah failed completely.

The woman then flees into the wilderness, where God feeds and protects her for 1,260 days. This is the same time period that keeps showing up in Revelation—forty-two months, three and a half years—symbolizing the entire era between Christ's ascension and his return. In the wilderness, God's people are not comfortable, but they are safe. Not spared from hardship, but sustained through it.

WAR IN HEAVEN

Now John sees the same battle from a different angle—the heavenly perspective. Michael the archangel and his angels fight against the dragon and his forces. The dragon loses. He isn't strong enough. He and his angels are thrown out of heaven and cast down to the earth.

What does this mean? This isn't a battle that happened before creation. It's a picture of what Christ accomplished through the cross and resurrection. When Jesus died and rose again, he broke the dragon's power to accuse God's people. Satan's most dangerous weapon was never persecution—it was accusation. He stood before God's throne day and night, pointing at believers and saying, "Look at them. They're sinners. They don't deserve your love. They're guilty."

But the blood of the Lamb silenced the accuser forever.

A loud voice in heaven shouts the good news: "Now the

salvation and the power and the kingdom of our God and the authority of his Christ have come, for the accuser of our brothers has been thrown down!" Then it explains how the saints conquer: "They overcame him by the blood of the Lamb and by the word of their testimony, for they loved not their lives even unto death."

Three weapons defeat the dragon. The blood of Jesus—his sacrifice that pays for sin and removes every accusation. The word of their testimony—the faithful witness of Christians who refuse to stay silent. And their willingness to die rather than deny their King.

But there's a warning built into the celebration: "Woe to the earth and the sea, for the devil has come down to you in great wrath, because he knows that his time is short!"

A defeated enemy with a short clock is the most dangerous kind. The dragon can no longer accuse Christians before God. So instead, he turns his fury on them on earth. He can't destroy their standing before God, so he tries to destroy their bodies, their faith, and their witness. That's what persecution is—the tantrum of a beaten enemy.

THE DRAGON'S FRUSTRATED RAGE

Cast down to earth, the dragon chases the woman. But God gives her "two wings of the great eagle" to fly to her wilderness refuge—language borrowed from the Exodus, when God told Israel, "I bore you on eagles' wings and brought you to myself." The dragon spews a river from his mouth to sweep her away—a flood of deception and lies meant to drown the church's faith. But the earth opens up and swallows the river. God intervenes.

Twice thwarted—unable to destroy the child and unable to drown the mother—the dragon turns his rage toward "the rest of her offspring, who keep the commandments of God and hold to the testimony of Jesus." That's the church. That's you, if you belong to Jesus. The dragon hates you because you belong to the one who beat him. And to wage this war, he calls up reinforcements.

THE BEAST FROM THE SEA

The dragon stands on the shore, and out of the sea rises a beast. In the ancient world, the sea represented chaos and evil—the untamed, dangerous deep. This beast is terrifying: ten horns, seven heads, and on each horn a crown. Its body combines features from Daniel's four beasts—a leopard, a bear, and a lion—representing the accumulated power of every godless empire in history: Babylon, Persia, Greece, and Rome.

The dragon gives this beast his own throne and authority. The sea beast is the dragon's political agent—worldly power animated by satanic ambition. In John's day, this was Rome. But the beast is bigger than Rome. It's every government, every system, every empire that demands the worship that belongs to God alone.

One of the beast's heads has a fatal wound that has healed. The whole earth marvels at this and worships the beast. This is a deliberate mockery of Christ. Jesus was slain and rose again. The beast imitates that pattern—a counterfeit death and resurrection designed to steal the Lamb's glory. The world looks at this imitation and asks, "Who is like the beast, and who can fight against it?" That question is a twisted echo of Israel's worship song: "Who is like the Lord?"

The beast speaks arrogant, blasphemous words. It wages war on the saints and conquers them—physically, not spiritually. It rules for forty-two months. And everyone on earth whose name is not written in the Lamb's book of life worships it.

Then comes the call that defines the church's response: "Here is a call for the endurance and faith of the saints." Not violence. Not political power. Not retaliation. Endurance and faith. That's how God's people respond to the beast. They outlast it. They out-trust it. They refuse to bow, even when bowing would save their lives.

THE BEAST FROM THE EARTH

A second beast rises, this time from the land. It looks like a lamb—two small horns, harmless appearance—but it speaks like a dragon. This is the false prophet, the religious and cultural arm of the dragon's operation. If the first beast is the fist, the second beast is the whisper.

This beast performs great signs. It calls fire from heaven, imitating Elijah. It gives breath to an image of the first beast, mimicking the Spirit who gives life to Christian. It's a counterfeit miracle worker, using impressive displays to convince people that the first beast deserves their worship.

Together, the dragon and the two beasts form an unholy trinity—a grotesque parody of the Father, Son, and Holy Spirit. The dragon mimics God the Father, the authority behind everything. The sea beast mimics Christ, the powerful one who "died" and "rose again." The earth beast mimics the Holy Spirit, pointing people toward the false christ and performing signs to validate its claims.

The false prophet forces everyone—rich and poor, free and enslaved—to receive a mark on their right hand or forehead. Without this mark, no one can buy or sell. The mark represents allegiance. Just as God's people are sealed on their foreheads with his name, the beast's followers are marked with the beast's name. The forehead represents what you think; the right hand represents what you do. The mark of the beast is total loyalty—letting a power other than God control your mind and your actions.

John closes with a riddle: "Let the one who has understanding calculate the number of the beast, for it is the number of a man, and his number is 666."

Throughout history, people have tried to decode this number as a specific person. The most likely original reference is to Nero Caesar, whose name, when written in Hebrew letters, adds up to 666. But the deeper meaning goes beyond one emperor. Seven is the number of completeness and perfection in Revelation. Six falls short of seven. And 666 is six repeated three times—a triple failure, a parody of the divine that can never reach it. The beast tries to be God. It always falls short.

WHAT THIS MEANS FOR US

First, the real enemy is behind the curtain. When life gets hard for Christians—when culture mocks faith, when governments pressure believers, when lies about God spread—Revelation says there's a reason. Behind every visible opposition stands an invisible dragon. That doesn't mean we should see demons behind every problem. But it does mean we should understand that the struggle is spiritual, and the weapons that win are spiritual too: the blood of the Lamb, the word of our testimony, and a willingness to follow Jesus no matter the cost.

Second, the dragon is defeated, not dead. Satan lost the decisive battle at the cross. He can no longer accuse believers before God. But he still rages on earth, and his time is short. That explains why evil sometimes feels so intense—it's the fury of an enemy who knows the clock is ticking. Don't mistake his rage for strength. He's thrashing because he's losing.

Third, the beast demands what only God deserves. Whenever any system—political, cultural, economic—demands total loyalty, it's acting like the beast. Whenever someone says, "This is the only thing that matters; give it everything you have," and that thing isn't God, the beast's pattern is at work. The call for God's people is always the same: endurance and faith. Refuse to worship anything with the Lamb's throne room address on it that isn't actually the Lamb.

Fourth, counterfeits only work if you don't know the real thing. The unholy trinity succeeds by imitation. The beast looks like the Lamb. The false prophet performs signs like the Spirit. The only way to see through the counterfeit is to know the original. The deeper you know Jesus—his character, his Word, his cross—the harder it is for any imitation to fool you.

TALKING POINTS

1. **The dragon has been fighting against God's people since Genesis 3.** How does knowing the conflict is that old help you understand what the church faces today?

2. **The saints overcome the dragon "by the blood of the Lamb, the word of their testimony, and not loving their lives**

even unto death." What does each of those three weapons look like in your life?

3. **The earth beast looks like a lamb but speaks like a dragon.** Why is deception more dangerous than force? How can you tell the difference between a true and false message?

4. **The mark of the beast is about allegiance—what controls your thinking and your actions.** What things compete with God for your total loyalty?

5. **The number 666 represents falling short of God's perfection.** How does that help you understand what evil really is—not an equal opposite of God, but a cheap imitation?

The dragon is raging. The beasts are prowling. But the Lamb is still on his throne, and his people are still sealed. The next chapter of John's vision will reveal the Lamb standing on Mount Zion with his army—not warriors carrying swords, but worshipers carrying a song. And it will show what happens when God's patience finally reaches its end.

Turn the page.

7

THE HARVEST AND THE BOWLS

In *Avatar: The Last Airbender*, there's a recurring pattern: just when it looks like the Fire Nation has won—just when the heroes are scattered, outmatched, and on the verge of giving up—the story pulls back and shows you something you forgot. The Avatar is still alive. The resistance is still standing. And the final battle is coming, not on the Fire Lord's terms, but on theirs.

Revelation 14 does exactly this. After two chapters of dragons and beasts, after the mark and the number and the war on the saints, John lifts his eyes—and the very first thing he sees is the Lamb, standing on Mount Zion, surrounded by 144,000 people with his name written on their foreheads. Not the beast's mark. The Lamb's name.

The dragon raged. The beasts blasphemed. And the Lamb's people are still standing.

From here, Revelation moves toward its climax. Three angels deliver urgent messages. Two harvests separate the faithful from the rebellious. Heaven sings one last song. And then seven bowls of final judgment are poured out on a world that refused to repent. These chapters are intense—but they are not hopeless. They are the story of a God who finishes what he starts, who answers the prayers of his suffering people, and who will not let evil have the last word.

THE LAMB AND THE 144,000

Chapter 13 ended with the beast's number—666. Chapter 14 opens with the Lamb's army—144,000. That contrast is deliberate. The beast's followers bear his mark on their foreheads and hands. The Lamb's followers bear his name and his Father's name on their foreheads. Two marks. Two loyalties. Two completely different futures.

The 144,000 stand on Mount Zion—the mountain of God's presence, the heart of his kingdom. These are the same people we met in chapter 7: the complete number of God's redeemed, sealed and preserved through every trial. They are not cowering in a corner. They are standing with their King.

And they are singing. A sound comes from heaven "like the roar of many waters and like the sound of loud thunder"—and also like the music of harpists playing their instruments. It is a new song, and no one can learn it except the 144,000. This isn't just music. It's the song of people who have been purchased by the Lamb's blood, who have followed him through suffering, and who have refused to trade their loyalty for comfort. You can only sing this song if you've lived it.

John calls them "firstfruits"—the first portion of the harvest offered to God, guaranteeing that the rest is coming. The 144,000 are proof that the full harvest of the redeemed will follow. The beast claimed the world's allegiance. The Lamb secured his people's souls. And they're still singing.

THREE ANGELS, THREE MESSAGES

The scene shifts to the sky, where three angels deliver messages that put the whole conflict into perspective.

The first angel flies across heaven carrying "an eternal gospel" and proclaims it to every nation, tribe, language, and people: "Fear God and give him glory, because the hour of his judgment has come, and worship him who made heaven and earth, the sea and the springs of water." This is the gospel in its simplest form—not a soft suggestion, but an urgent command. The same God who created everything is about to judge everything. The only sane response is to stop worshiping what he made and start worshiping him. In a world where the beast demands worship, this angel's message cuts through every lie: there is one Creator, and he alone deserves your allegiance.

The second angel announces what hasn't happened yet in the story but is already certain: "Fallen, fallen is Babylon the great, she who made all nations drink the wine of the passion of her sexual immorality." Babylon is Revelation's code name for the world system that seduces people away from God—not with brute force, but with luxury, pleasure, power, and pride. In John's day, Babylon meant Rome. But Babylon is bigger than Rome. It's any culture, economy, or system that intoxicates people with the promise that you can have everything you want without God. The angel speaks of Babylon's fall in the past tense even though it hasn't happened yet. That's how certain it is. In God's eyes, it's already done.

The third angel delivers the most sobering message: anyone who worships the beast and receives its mark will face God's wrath, undiluted and final. The imagery is severe—fire, sulfur, torment—and it's meant to be. John isn't describing punishment for the sake of cruelty. He's showing the ultimate consequence of choosing a counterfeit god over the real one. When you build your entire life on something that isn't God, the collapse of that thing is the collapse of everything.

Then comes the verse that ties it all together: "Here is a call for the endurance of the saints, those who keep the commandments of God and their faith in Jesus." There it is again. Endurance. Faith. In a world that offers Babylon's wine or the beast's mark, the church's calling is the same as it has been since chapter 1: hold on. Stay faithful. Don't let go.

And then a voice from heaven adds one more thing: "Blessed are the dead who die in the Lord from now on. They will rest from their labors, and their deeds will follow them." For Christians who face death rather than deny their King, this is the promise that seals everything: your suffering is not wasted. Your faithfulness follows you into eternity. Rest is coming.

TWO HARVESTS

Next, John sees someone sitting on a white cloud—"one like a son of man," with a golden crown and a sharp sickle. This echoes Daniel's vision of the Son of Man and Jesus' own teaching about the final judgment in Matthew 13, where he compared the end of the age to a harvest.

An angel calls out from the temple: "Put in your sickle and reap, for the hour to reap has come, for the harvest of the earth is fully ripe." The Son of Man swings his sickle, and the earth is harvested—this is the gathering of the righteous, the final ingathering of everyone who belongs to God.

Then a second angel appears with another sharp sickle, and a third angel—the one who has authority over fire—tells him to gather the grapes. These grapes are thrown into "the great winepress of the wrath of God." Blood flows from the winepress as high as a horse's bridle for 1,600 stadia—a number that symbolizes completeness (four squared times ten squared), meaning God's justice reaches everywhere and misses nothing.

The two harvests make the same point the three angels made: humanity faces a choice, and that choice has consequences. The grain harvest is salvation—being gathered by the Son of Man into God's presence. The grape harvest is judgment—the crushing weight of God's justice on everything that defied him. Revelation doesn't give us a comfortable middle ground. It gives us the Lamb or the beast, Zion or Babylon, the harvest of life or the winepress of wrath.

THE SONG OF MOSES AND THE LAMB

Before the final judgments fall, heaven pauses to worship. This happens again and again in Revelation—worship before wrath, singing before shaking. It's not accidental. It's the pattern: God's people worship first, and that worship gives them the strength to face whatever comes next.

John sees the redeemed standing beside a sea of glass mixed with fire—the same sea of glass from the throne room in chapter 4, but now shot through with the fire of God's purifying judgment. These people have conquered the beast. They refused the mark. They held on to the Lamb. And now they sing.

Their song is called "the song of Moses, the servant of God, and the song of the Lamb." That title ties two great moments of deliverance into one. When God rescued Israel from Egypt through the Red Sea, Moses led the people in a song of triumph. Now, the redeemed sing a new version of that same song—because the Lamb has accomplished a greater exodus, rescuing his people not from one empire but from the power of sin and death itself.

The lyrics declare, "Great and amazing are your deeds, O Lord God the Almighty! Just and true are your ways, O King of the nations! Who will not fear, O Lord, and glorify your name? For you alone are holy. All nations will come and worship you, for your righteous acts have been revealed." Notice what they're praising God for. Not just his mercy. His justice. His "righteous acts." The bowls of wrath that are about to be poured out are not contradictions of God's goodness—they are expressions of it. A God who ignored evil forever would not be good. He would be indifferent. The redeemed praise him because he is both merciful and just, and they trust him to get the balance exactly right.

THE SEVEN BOWLS

Now the heavenly temple opens, and seven angels emerge carrying seven golden bowls filled with the wrath of God. The temple fills with smoke from God's glory—so thick that no one can enter until the judgments are complete. The time for intercession is over. The time for final justice has come.

A loud voice from the temple commands, "Go and pour out on the earth the seven bowls of the wrath of God." The bowls echo the plagues of Egypt, but they are more intense than the trumpets. Where the trumpets affected a third, the bowls affect everything. The restraint is over. These are the final judgments.

The **first bowl** brings painful sores on everyone who bears the beast's mark. The **second** turns the entire sea to blood—"like the blood of a corpse"—and every living thing in it dies. The **third** turns the rivers and springs to blood. An angel declares, "Just are you, O Holy One, who is and who was, for you brought these judgments. For they have shed the blood of saints and prophets, and you have given them blood to drink. It is what they deserve." Even the altar responds: "Yes, Lord God the Almighty, true and just are your judgments."

The **fourth bowl** scorches people with fierce heat from the sun. Their response? "They cursed the name of God who had power over these plagues. They did not repent and give him glory." The **fifth bowl** plunges the beast's kingdom into darkness, and people gnaw their tongues in anguish—but still, "they did not repent of their deeds."

That refrain—"they did not repent"—is one of the saddest lines in the Bible. Trumpet after trumpet, bowl after bowl, the world is shaken, scorched, and darkened. And still, people cling to the beast instead of turning to the Lamb. It proves what Revelation has been saying all along: suffering alone does not change hearts. Only grace can do that. And grace must be received, not refused.

The **sixth bowl** dries up the Euphrates River—the ancient boundary between civilization and chaos—and three frog-like spirits emerge from the mouths of the dragon, the beast, and the false prophet. These demonic spirits perform signs that deceive the kings of the earth and gather them for battle at a place called Armageddon.

Armageddon isn't a spot on a map to circle in red. The name comes from Megiddo, an ancient battlefield in Israel where decisive conflicts were fought throughout the Old Testament. It represents the final showdown between the forces of evil and the God who rules. It's the moment every rebel kingdom has been building toward—and the moment that will end every one of them.

Right in the middle of this, Jesus speaks directly to his church: "Behold, I am coming like a thief! Blessed is the one who stays awake, keeping his garments on." Even at the edge of the final battle, the call is the same: stay alert. Stay faithful. Stay dressed and ready.

The **seventh bowl** is poured into the air, and a loud voice from the throne declares: "It is done." Those words echo through the whole Bible. On the cross, Jesus cried, "It is finished"—redemption accomplished. Now, from heaven's throne, the same God says, "It is done"—justice completed. Lightning, thunder, the worst earthquake in history, and hailstones weighing a hundred pounds. Babylon the great is split apart and remembered before God for judgment. The world's most powerful system, the one that intoxicated the nations with its luxury and pride, crumbles in a single moment.

And still—"they cursed God."

WHAT THIS MEANS FOR US

First, the Lamb's people will stand. No matter how fierce the dragon's rage or how persuasive the beast's propaganda, the 144,000 are still on Mount Zion, still singing, still bearing the Lamb's name. Your faithfulness will not be erased.

Second, God's justice is not cruelty—it's completion. The bowls are severe because evil is severe. A God who never judged would be a God who didn't care about the suffering of his people. The redeemed don't cringe at justice—they sing about it. "Just and true are your ways."

Third, repentance is a gift, not a guarantee. The saddest thread in these chapters is the repeated refusal to repent. Judgment alone can't soften a hard heart. Only the Spirit of God can do that. If you feel the pull to turn back to God—respond. That pull is grace, and it won't last forever.

Fourth, "It is done" is a promise, not a threat. For those who belong to the Lamb, the seventh bowl is not the end of hope. It's the beginning of restoration. When God says "It is done," he means evil has been dealt with. Justice has been served. Now the way is clear for everything to be made new.

TALKING POINTS

1. **Chapter 14 opens with the Lamb and the 144,000 right after the beast's worst threats.** Why do you think John placed this scene here? What does it tell us about the outcome of the conflict?

2. **The first angel proclaims "an eternal gospel" to every nation.** What makes the gospel both good news and an urgent warning?

3. **The redeemed sing "the song of Moses and the Lamb."** What do the exodus from Egypt and the cross of Jesus have in common?

4. **The bowls are more severe than the trumpets—no more "a third," now it's everything.** What does that escalation tell us about God's patience and his justice?

5. **People refuse to repent even under the bowls.** Why do you think suffering alone doesn't change hearts? What does change them?

The bowls have been poured. Babylon has cracked. The voice from the throne has spoken. But Babylon's full story hasn't been told yet. John is about to see the great city in all its seductive glory—and then watch it burn. The fall of everything the world worshiped is next.

Turn the page.

8

THE FALL OF BABYLON

In *The Wizard of Oz*, everyone in the Emerald City is terrified of the Great and Powerful Oz. His voice booms through the throne room. His face looms above them, wreathed in fire and smoke. He seems unstoppable, all-knowing, and worthy of total obedience. But then Toto pulls back the curtain—and behind all that spectacle is just an ordinary man pulling levers and speaking into a microphone. The whole thing was an illusion. The power was fake. The glory was manufactured.

Revelation 17–18 is the moment the curtain gets pulled back on the world's most convincing illusion. Throughout this book, John has shown his readers the dragon and the beasts—the spiritual forces behind the world's rebellion against God. Now he introduces one more character: a woman called Babylon. She isn't a warrior. She isn't a monster. She's something more dangerous than either. She is beautiful, wealthy, dazzling, and intoxicating. She doesn't conquer people with swords. She seduces them with luxury. She doesn't demand worship at swordpoint like the beast. She makes people want to worship the world all on their own—because she makes the world look so good.

But John pulls back the curtain. And behind Babylon's gold and jewels, behind her perfume and power, he finds blood—the blood of prophets, saints, and martyrs. Her beauty hides brutality. Her wealth was built on the backs of the exploited. And her downfall, when it comes, is total, sudden, and irreversible.

The great city falls. And the question for God's people is the same one it's always been: Which city do you belong to?

THE WOMAN ON THE BEAST

One of the bowl angels invites John to come see something: "the judgment of the great prostitute who is seated on many waters." In the Bible, prostitution is often used as an image for spiritual unfaithfulness—for people or nations that abandon God and chase after other loyalties. That's what Babylon does. She lures the nations away from God through seduction, not force.

John is carried in the Spirit to a wilderness, and there he sees a woman sitting on a scarlet beast—the same seven-headed, ten-horned beast from chapter 13. The beast carries her. The beast supports her. The connection is deliberate: Babylon's luxury and the beast's political power work together. Seduction and coercion are partners. One offers the carrot; the other carries the stick.

The woman herself is stunning. She wears purple and scarlet—the colors of royalty and wealth. She glitters with gold, jewels, and pearls. In her hand she holds a golden cup. But the cup isn't filled with something precious. It's filled with "abominations and the impurities of her sexual immorality." The outside is gorgeous; the inside is poison.

On her forehead is a name: "Babylon the great, mother of prostitutes and of earth's abominations." And she is drunk—not on wine, but on "the blood of the saints, the blood of the martyrs of Jesus."

That's the real Babylon. Beneath the glitter, she's a murderer. Behind the luxury, she's a destroyer. She looks like a queen, but she acts like a predator. And the nations are too intoxicated by her wealth to notice.

WHAT BABYLON REPRESENTS

So who is Babylon? For John's first readers, the answer was obvious: Rome. Rome was the city on seven hills (and the angel actually says the seven heads represent seven hills). Rome was the empire that seduced the world with its wealth, culture, roads, and entertainment—while simultaneously persecuting Christians who refused to worship the emperor.

But Babylon is bigger than Rome. She always has been.

The original Babylon was the ancient city in Genesis 11 where humanity tried to build a tower to heaven—a monument to their own greatness. Throughout the Old Testament, Babylon became the symbol of every civilization that glorifies itself instead of God. And in Revelation, Babylon represents the world's seductive system in every century—the culture that says, "You don't need God. You have money. You have comfort. You have entertainment. You have power. What else could you possibly want?"

Babylon is the golden cup that looks beautiful but poisons everyone who drinks from it. She's the system that trades in luxuries while also trading in "human souls" (18:13). She's the economy that enriches the powerful by crushing the vulnerable. She's the voice that whispers to every generation: "This world is all there is, so take everything you can get."

She isn't one city. She's a spirit that possesses every city that forgets God.

THE BEAST TURNS ON THE WOMAN

The angel reveals something shocking: the beast and its allies will eventually turn on Babylon and destroy her. The very political powers that carried her and benefited from her luxury will "hate the prostitute. They will make her desolate and naked, and devour her flesh and burn her up with fire."

Evil consumes itself. The alliances built on greed and ambition always collapse, because greed and ambition don't know how to be loyal. The kings who drank from Babylon's cup will eventually smash it—not because they've repented, but because selfishness eventually turns on everything, including its own partners.

And behind it all, God is at work. "God has put it into their hearts to carry out his purpose." Even the self-destruction of evil serves God's plan. He doesn't just oppose Babylon—he allows Babylon to undo itself. That's how thorough his sovereignty is.

The angel concludes with a line that would have sent chills down every Roman spine: "The woman that you saw is the great city that has dominion over the kings of the earth." In John's day, there was only one city that fit that description. But the point goes beyond Rome. Every great city that dominates the world through wealth and power eventually meets the same end. Babylon always falls.

FALLEN, FALLEN IS BABYLON THE GREAT

Chapter 18 opens with another angel descending from heaven, blazing with glory so bright that the whole earth is lit up. His message is devastating: "Fallen, fallen is Babylon the great!" He says it twice because there's no doubt. Babylon's fall isn't a possibility; it's a certainty. In God's eyes, it's already done.

The angel describes what Babylon has become: a dwelling place for demons, a haunt for unclean spirits, a cage for every detestable bird. The city that glittered with gold is now a ruin haunted by evil. All the nations that drank her wine, all the kings who shared her luxury, all the merchants who grew rich from her excess—none of them can save her now.

Then comes one of the most important commands in the entire book: "Come out of her, my people, lest you take part in her sins, lest you share in her plagues." God isn't saying, "Move to a different zip code." He's saying, "Don't let her values become your values." The danger for Christians has never been just persecution from the outside. It's also seduction from the inside—the slow, quiet compromise that happens when God's people start living like Babylon instead of living like the Lamb. "Come out of her" means: stop drinking from her cup. Stop measuring success the way she does. Stop worshiping what she worships. You can live in the world without belonging to it.

Babylon's pride is breathtaking. She says in her heart: "I sit as queen, I am no widow, and mourning I shall never see." She believes she's untouchable. She believes her luxury will last forever. She's wrong. "In a single day her plagues will come—death and mourning and famine—and she will be burned up with fire, for mighty is the Lord God who has judged her." The city that thought it would never fall—falls in a single day.

THREE LAMENTS

When Babylon burns, three groups stand at a distance, watching the smoke rise. Each one mourns, but not for the right reasons.

The kings of the earth weep because they've lost their partner in power. They shared in her luxury, played her political games, and benefited from her influence. Now it's gone. They cry, "Alas, alas, you great city, you mighty city Babylon! For in a single hour your judgment has come."

The merchants of the earth weep because they've lost their customers. John lists their cargo in devastating detail: gold, silver, jewels, pearls, fine linen, purple cloth, silk, scarlet fabric, fragrant wood, ivory, bronze, iron, marble, cinnamon, spice, incense, myrrh, frankincense, wine, oil, fine flour, wheat, cattle, sheep, horses, chariots—and at the very end, almost as an afterthought, "slaves, that is, human souls."

That last item exposes everything. Babylon's economy was willing to sell people. In a list of luxury goods, human beings are just another product. That's what happens when a culture worships wealth: people become merchandise. Greed always dehumanizes.

The merchants don't mourn the injustice. They mourn the profit. "The fruit for which your soul longed has gone from you, and all your delicacies and your splendors are lost to you, never to be found again!"

The sailors and sea traders weep because the shipping lanes

have gone silent. The global economy that made them rich has collapsed overnight. They throw dust on their heads and cry, "What city was like the great city?"

Notice: all three groups stand "far off." They don't rush in to help. They don't try to save Babylon. They just watch her burn and cry about what they've lost. That's what Babylon's relationships look like—everyone is connected by profit, and when the profit ends, so does the loyalty.

HEAVEN REJOICES

Earth mourns. But heaven sings. "Rejoice over her, O heaven, and you saints and apostles and prophets, for God has given judgment for you against her!"

This isn't gloating. It's vindication. Remember the martyrs under the altar in chapter 6, crying, "How long, O Lord?" Remember the blood of the saints that Babylon drank like wine? Those prayers have been answered. Those deaths have been avenged. God's justice has arrived—not as revenge, but as the long-promised setting-right of everything Babylon corrupted.

For God's people, Babylon's fall isn't the end of hope. It's the beginning of freedom. The system that exploited, seduced, and murdered the faithful is finally, permanently, irreversibly done.

THE MILLSTONE

The chapter closes with one final, unforgettable image. A mighty angel picks up a stone the size of a great millstone and hurls it into the sea. "So will Babylon the great city be thrown down with violence, and will be found no more."

Then comes a haunting list of everything that will disappear from Babylon—forever: No more music. No more craftsmen. No more grinding of grain. No more lamplight. No more weddings. No more voice of the bride and groom.

Six times the phrase "no more" echoes through the passage, like a bell tolling for a funeral. Everything that made a city feel alive—art, work, food, light, love—is gone. Not temporarily. Not for a season. Forever.

Why? "For your merchants were the great ones of the earth, and all nations were deceived by your sorcery. And in her was found the blood of prophets and of saints, and of all who have been slain on earth." That's the verdict. Babylon fell because she deceived the nations, enriched herself on exploitation, and murdered God's people. The most dazzling civilization on earth crumbled because it was built on lies, greed, and blood.

The silence after the music is the most powerful sound in these two chapters. Babylon is finally quiet. And into that silence, heaven's song will begin.

WHAT THIS MEANS FOR US

First, Babylon is still pouring drinks. We don't live in first-century Rome, but Babylon's golden cup is still being offered. Every culture that says "Buy more, consume more, achieve more, and you'll be happy" is speaking Babylon's language. Every system that values profit over people, luxury over justice, or image over integrity carries Babylon's name. Recognizing her voice is the first step to resisting it.

Second, "Come out of her" is a daily choice. You can't physically leave the culture you live in—and God doesn't ask you to. But you can refuse to drink from her cup. You can choose generosity over greed, faithfulness over fame, and the Lamb's values over the world's. "Coming out" means being present in the world without being possessed by it.

Third, evil destroys itself. The beast turns on Babylon. The allies betray each other. The system collapses under its own corruption. Sin doesn't just offend God—it eats itself alive. Every empire built on injustice carries the seeds of its own destruction.

Fourth, God's justice answers the martyrs' prayers. The fall of Babylon is heaven's response to "How long, O Lord?" It's proof that God heard every prayer, counted every tear, and remembered every drop of blood. Justice may be slow by our clocks, but it is certain by his.

Fifth, the Lamb's kingdom will outlast every Babylon. Rome fell. Every empire that followed has fallen or will fall. The only kingdom that never ends is the one built on the cross. When every golden cup has shattered and every great city has gone silent, the Lamb's people will still be singing.

TALKING POINTS

1. **Babylon seduces rather than attacks.** Why is seduction sometimes more dangerous for Christians than persecution?

2. **The merchants' cargo list ends with "slaves, that is, human souls."** How does that detail expose what happens when wealth becomes an idol?

3. **"Come out of her, my people" doesn't mean leave the world—it means don't live by the world's values.** What does that look like practically for you?

4. **Heaven rejoices while earth mourns.** How can both reactions be appropriate at the same time?

5. **The "no more" list includes music, light, weddings, and craftsmanship—good things.** Why does Babylon's fall silence even good things? What made Babylon's version of those things corrupted?

Babylon has fallen. The golden cup is shattered. The great city is silent. But the story isn't over—it's about to become the most joyful it's ever been. Heaven is preparing for a wedding, a rider is about to appear on a white horse, and the one who conquered by dying is about to conquer for the final time.

Turn the page.

9

THE WEDDING, THE RIDER, AND THE END OF EVIL

In *The Return of the King*—the final volume of *The Lord of the Rings*—there's a moment when everything changes. The ring is destroyed. Sauron falls. The eagles arrive. And then Aragorn, who has spent the entire story in exile, walking through danger and darkness, is crowned king. The battle is over. The throne is filled. The wedding comes. And everyone who suffered through the long defeat finally sees that their faithfulness was worth it.

Revelation 19–20 is the Bible's version of that moment—except it's not fiction. Babylon has fallen. The smoke of the great city still rises. And now heaven opens, not with another judgment or another warning, but with something the whole book has been building toward: a celebration. A wedding. A rider on a white horse. And the final, permanent defeat of every enemy that ever stood against the Lamb and his people.

These chapters answer the question that has hung over the entire book: How does the story end? The answer comes in three movements: heaven sings, the Lamb conquers, and evil is destroyed—completely, permanently, and forever.

HEAVEN EXPLODES WITH PRAISE

The first sound John hears after Babylon's fall is not silence. It's a roar. "Hallelujah! Salvation and glory and power belong to our God, for his judgments are true and just; for he has judged the great prostitute who corrupted the earth with her immorality, and has avenged on her the blood of his servants."

"Hallelujah" is a Hebrew word that means "Praise the Lord!" It appears four times in these opening verses—the only place in the entire New Testament where this word is used. Heaven isn't whispering. Heaven is shouting. Four hallelujahs, one after another, praising God for justice, for victory, for righteousness, and for the fact that the Lamb is about to reign without rival forever.

Notice what heaven is celebrating. Not destruction for its own sake. Not revenge. Heaven is praising God because truth has won. Because the system that murdered the saints and corrupted the earth has been judged. Because righteousness—finally, fully—has prevailed.

The twenty-four elders and the four living creatures fall down and worship: "Amen. Hallelujah!" And then a voice from the throne calls everyone to join: "Praise our God, all you his servants, you who fear him, small and great."

What follows is the sound John has been hearing pieces of throughout the entire book, but now it reaches its fullest volume: "like the roar of many waters and like the sound of mighty peals of thunder." And the words are these: "Hallelujah! For the Lord our God the Almighty reigns."

He reigns. That's been the message of every seal, every trumpet, every bowl, every vision. And now it's declared with nothing standing in the way.

THE MARRIAGE OF THE LAMB

The celebration shifts from a courtroom to a wedding. "Let us rejoice and exult and give him the glory, for the marriage of the Lamb has come, and his Bride has made herself ready."

Throughout the Bible, God's relationship with his people is described as a marriage. The prophets called Israel God's bride. Paul called the church the bride of Christ. The whole Bible has been a love story—a covenant between a faithful God and a people he refused to give up on, no matter how many times they wandered.

Now the wedding day has arrived. The long engagement is over. The Bride—the church—is dressed and ready. Her gown is "fine linen, bright and pure," which John explains represents "the righteous deeds of the saints." But even this dress is a gift. She didn't earn it. She was given it by the Groom whose sacrifice made her clean.

An angel tells John: "Blessed are those who are invited to the marriage supper of the Lamb."

John is so overwhelmed that he falls at the angel's feet to worship him. The angel immediately stops him: "You must not do that! I am a fellow servant with you. Worship God."

Even in the most glorious moment of the entire vision, the rule hasn't changed: worship belongs to God alone. Not to angels. Not to messengers. Not to any created thing. Only to the Lamb.

The wedding feast is the ultimate destination of God's people—not escape from the world, but eternal union with Christ. Everything the church has endured—every persecution, every temptation, every season of suffering—was the journey to this table.

THE RIDER ON THE WHITE HORSE

Then heaven opens again. And this time, what comes out is not a voice or a song. It's a warrior. "Then I saw heaven opened, and behold, a white horse! The one sitting on it is called Faithful and True, and in righteousness he judges and makes war."

This is Jesus. Not the gentle teacher of Galilee, though he is that too. This is the risen, reigning, victorious King—the one the whole universe has been waiting for. His eyes are like a flame of fire. On his head are many crowns—more than the dragon's seven, more than the beast's ten. He wears a robe dipped in blood—not his enemies' blood, but his own. The blood of the cross. The blood that won the victory.

His name is "The Word of God." And from his mouth comes a sharp sword—not a metal blade, but the word of truth, the same word that created the universe and that now judges the nations.

Behind him ride the armies of heaven, dressed in white linen on white horses. But notice something remarkable: none of them carry weapons. The battle belongs entirely to the King. His word is enough. His truth does all the fighting. The saints don't conquer by violence. They conquer because they follow the one whose word is sharper than any sword ever forged.

On his robe and on his thigh is written a name: "King of kings and Lord of lords." Every title the beast claimed, every crown the dragon wore, every boast the false prophet made— all of it was a counterfeit of this. There is one King above all kings. One Lord above all lords. And he rides not to enslave but to liberate. Not to destroy for pleasure but to end the reign of everything that destroyed his people.

The beast and the false prophet are captured and thrown alive into the lake of fire. Their followers are struck down by the sword from his mouth. The birds feast on the remains. The battle is over almost before it begins.

That's the pattern throughout Revelation. Evil builds up slowly, gathering power and allies, making grand speeches and performing impressive signs. But when it meets the Lamb, it collapses in an instant. Every empire that sets itself against God follows the same script: a long rise and a sudden fall.

THE BINDING OF THE DRAGON

With the beast and false prophet destroyed, one enemy remains: the dragon himself.

An angel descends from heaven carrying a key and a great chain. He seizes the dragon—"that ancient serpent, who is the devil and Satan"—and binds him for a thousand years. He throws him into the abyss, locks it, and seals it over him. The purpose of the binding is specific: "so that he might not deceive the nations any longer."

Now, this thousand years—the "millennium"—has been the subject of more debate than almost any other passage in the Bible. People have argued for centuries about whether it's a literal thousand-year period in the future or a symbolic picture of something else. Here's what we can say with confidence, based on the rest of Revelation's approach to numbers.

Throughout Revelation, numbers are symbolic. Seven means completeness. Twelve means the people of God. 144,000 means all of God's redeemed. In the same way, a thousand represents an enormous, full, complete period of time.

The millennium represents the era between Christ's first coming and his return—the present age, the age of the church, the time we are living in right now.

When did the binding begin? When Jesus conquered the dragon through his death and resurrection. Remember chapter 12: the dragon was thrown out of heaven when Christ ascended to the throne. Jesus himself said, "I saw Satan fall like lightning from heaven" and spoke of "binding the strong man." The dragon's power has been restrained since the cross. He cannot prevent the gospel from spreading to every nation. He cannot assemble a final, worldwide attack against the church— yet. He still operates, but on a leash. His deception is limited. His time is measured.

During this same period, John sees thrones—and seated on them are the souls of those "who had been beheaded for the testimony of Jesus and for the word of God." These are the martyrs and faithful believers who refused to worship the beast. They "came to life and reigned with Christ for a thousand years." This is called "the first resurrection."

The "first resurrection" doesn't mean these people received their final, physical resurrection bodies. It means that even in death, they are alive with Christ, sharing his reign, vindicated before the throne. The world thought it killed them. Heaven says they're ruling. The beast thought it conquered them. The Lamb says they've conquered. Over those who share in this first resurrection, "the second death has no power"—meaning eternal separation from God can never touch them.

This is the reality the church lives in right now. Christ reigns. The saints share in his reign through faith, witness, and perseverance. The dragon is bound. The gospel advances. And the church endures, knowing that the present age—however long it lasts—is held firmly in the Lamb's hands.

THE FINAL REBELLION

When the thousand years are complete, Satan is released for a short time. He goes out to deceive the nations one last time, gathering them for a final assault against God's people. These nations are called "Gog and Magog"—names borrowed from the prophet Ezekiel, representing the collective enemies of God's people throughout history, gathered for one ultimate attack.

Their number is "like the sand of the sea." They surround "the camp of the saints and the beloved city." It looks hopeless. It looks like the end.

And then—fire from heaven consumes them.

No battle. No long siege. No desperate last stand. Just fire. Just God. Evil's final rebellion is crushed in a single sentence.

The devil is thrown into the lake of fire, where the beast and false prophet already wait. "And they will be tormented day and night forever and ever." The enemy who deceived the world from the garden of Eden to the end of history is finished. Not defeated temporarily. Not locked away to return again. Finished. Permanently. Eternally. The serpent's story is over.

THE GREAT WHITE THRONE

Now John sees the most solemn scene in the Bible. "Then I saw a great white throne and him who was seated on it. From his presence earth and sky fled away, and no place was found for them."

The entire created order shrinks back before the holiness of the one on the throne. There is nowhere to hide. No mountain to crawl under. No sea to swallow you. Everything is exposed.

"And I saw the dead, great and small, standing before the throne, and books were opened." Books of deeds. Every action, every choice, every hidden thing—recorded and revealed. No one is exempt. Rich and poor, powerful and forgotten, famous and unknown. Everyone stands before the same throne.

But there is another book: the book of life. The books of deeds show what people have done. The book of life shows who belongs to the Lamb. And the book of life is the one that matters most. Those whose names are written in it are safe—not because their record is perfect, but because the Lamb's blood covers every page. Their names were written by grace, secured by sacrifice, and kept by the one who holds all things.

"If anyone's name was not found written in the book of life, he was thrown into the lake of fire." This is called "the second death." The first death is the physical death every human being experiences. The second death is eternal separation from God—the final consequence of choosing the beast over the Lamb, Babylon over Zion, the dragon's lie over the Creator's truth.

And then something beautiful happens. "Death and Hades were thrown into the lake of fire." Death itself dies. The last enemy is destroyed. The thing that has haunted every human life since Genesis 3—the shadow that hung over every funeral, every goodbye, every tear—is gone. Not managed. Not reduced. Gone.

Creation is now ready for something it has been groaning for since the fall.

WHAT THIS MEANS FOR US

First, worship is the victory song. The four hallelujahs remind us that worship isn't just something we do on Sundays. It's how heaven responds to victory. Every time you worship—every prayer, every song, every act of trust—you are joining heaven's chorus and declaring that the Lamb reigns.

Second, the Lamb conquers by his word, not by our weapons. The rider on the white horse carries a sword in his mouth, not in his hand. Truth is his weapon. The church's job is not to overpower the world with force but to follow the Lamb and speak his truth with faithfulness and courage.

Third, the dragon is bound, but not yet destroyed. We live in the time between the binding and the lake of fire. Evil is real, but it's restrained. The gospel goes to every nation because the dragon cannot stop it. Take courage—the leash is shorter than it looks.

Fourth, your name in the book of life is what matters most. The great white throne judges according to deeds, but the book of life saves according to grace. Your standing before God doesn't depend on a perfect record. It depends on whether the Lamb's blood has covered you and whether his name is written over yours.

Fifth, death will die. The second-to-last enemy destroyed in Revelation isn't a beast or a dragon—it's death itself. For everyone who belongs to the Lamb, death is temporary. The second death has no power over you. And on the other side of the throne, a new world is waiting.

TALKING POINTS

1. **Heaven sings four hallelujahs after Babylon falls.** Why is praise the first response to victory? What does that tell us about the role of worship in the Christian life?

2. **The Bride's wedding dress is described as "the righteous deeds of the saints," yet it's also described as "given to her."** How can it be both earned and given?

3. **The rider on the white horse has a sword in his mouth, and his armies carry no weapons.** What does this tell us about how Jesus wins?

4. **At the great white throne, there are books of deeds and a book of life.** What's the difference between being judged by your deeds and being saved by grace?

5. **Death itself is thrown into the lake of fire.** What does it mean for you that the last enemy will be permanently destroyed?

The dragon is destroyed. The beast is finished. Death is dead. The throne has judged. And now, for the first time in the entire Bible, there is nothing left standing between God and his people. No sin. No curse. No enemy. No death. The stage is clear—and what John sees next is the most beautiful thing any human being has ever been shown.

Turn the page.

10

EVERYTHING NEW

At the end of *The Chronicles of Narnia*, something extraordinary happens. The old Narnia is destroyed—the stars fall, the sun goes out, the land freezes and floods and disappears. The children think everything they loved is gone forever. But then Aslan leads them through a door, and on the other side they find a new Narnia—brighter, deeper, more real, more alive than anything they've ever seen. Every good thing they loved about the old world is there, but more itself than before. "The things that began to happen after that," C. S. Lewis writes, "were so great and beautiful that I cannot write them."

That's exactly what happens at the end of Revelation. For twenty chapters, John has shown his readers a world at war— dragons and beasts, seals and trumpets, Babylon's seduction and heaven's judgment. The church has endured. The Lamb has conquered. The dragon is destroyed. Death itself has been thrown into the lake of fire. And now, with every enemy defeated and every sin judged, John lifts his eyes one last time.

And what he sees is not destruction. It's renewal. Not escape from the world, but the world made right. Not a farewell to creation, but creation's homecoming. The Bible's story began in a garden. It ends in a city. And in between, a Lamb made everything new.

A NEW HEAVEN AND A NEW EARTH

"Then I saw a new heaven and a new earth, for the first heaven and the first earth had passed away, and the sea was no more." The old creation—scarred by sin, groaning under the curse, stained by centuries of rebellion—is gone. But what replaces it isn't a blank canvas. The word "new" here doesn't mean "different" or "other." It means renewed, restored, transformed. This is the same creation, but gloriously healed. Every stain removed. Every fracture mended. Every dormant beauty brought to full bloom.

And the sea is no more. Throughout Revelation, the sea represented chaos, danger, and the source of evil—the beast rose from the sea, the restless waters symbolized the turmoil of the nations. In the new creation, there is no more chaos. No more threat. No more restless anxiety about what might rise from the deep. Peace, all the way down.

Then John sees the centerpiece of the new creation: "the holy city, new Jerusalem, coming down out of heaven from God, prepared as a bride adorned for her husband." Heaven doesn't stay up. It comes down. God doesn't pull his people out of creation—he brings his presence into it. The separation between heaven and earth that has defined human existence since the garden is healed. The two become one, and God makes his home with humanity.

A voice from the throne speaks the words the entire Bible has been building toward: "Behold, the dwelling place of

God is with man. He will dwell with them, and they will be his people, and God himself will be with them as their God." This is the promise that echoes from Genesis to Exodus to the prophets to the Psalms: "I will be your God, and you will be my people." It was whispered at Sinai, sung in the temple, and hoped for through every exile. Now it is fully, permanently, irreversibly true. No veil. No distance. No separation. God with his people, face to face, forever.

"He will wipe away every tear from their eyes, and death shall be no more, neither shall there be mourning, nor crying, nor pain anymore, for the former things have passed away." Every tear. Not just the big ones from tragedy and persecution. Every quiet tear of loneliness, disappointment, grief, and loss. God himself—not an angel, not a messenger, but God—wipes them away with his own hand. And death, the enemy that has stalked every page of human history, is no more. The thing that made every goodbye painful and every love bittersweet is gone.

Then the one on the throne speaks directly—one of the only times in Revelation when God the Father's own voice is heard: "Behold, I am making all things new." Not "all new things." All things new. The difference matters. God isn't scrapping creation and starting over. He's taking everything that was broken and restoring it. The same world, the same people, the same creation—but healed, glorified, and filled with his presence.

And then: "It is done! I am the Alpha and the Omega, the beginning and the end. To the thirsty I will give from the spring of the water of life without payment." From beginning to end—from the first word of creation to the last word of renewal—it's all his. And the water of life is free. Grace was free at the start, and grace is free at the finish.

THE HOLY CITY

One of the bowl angels—the same kind of angel who showed John Babylon's corruption—now shows him the Bride. The contrast is deliberate. Babylon was a prostitute, dazzling on the outside, rotten on the inside. The new Jerusalem is a bride, radiant with the kind of beauty that comes from holiness, not from hiding something ugly beneath a golden surface.

John is carried to a great, high mountain, and from there he sees the holy city descending from heaven, shining with the glory of God. Its radiance is "like a most rare jewel, like jasper, clear as crystal."

The city's dimensions are staggering. It measures twelve thousand stadia in every direction—length, width, and height. It's a perfect cube. That shape would have immediately reminded John's readers of one thing: the Holy of Holies—the innermost room of the temple, where God's presence dwelled, where only the high priest could enter once a year. The Holy of Holies was a cube. Now the entire city is shaped like it. What was once a single hidden room is now the shape of all reality. God's presence isn't confined to a sacred space anymore. It fills everything.

The city's twelve gates bear the names of the twelve tribes of Israel. Its twelve foundations bear the names of the twelve apostles. Old Testament and New Testament, Israel and the church, united in one structure. The walls gleam with jasper. The foundations flash with every precious stone imaginable—

sapphire, emerald, topaz, amethyst. The gates are pearls. The streets are gold so pure it looks like glass.

And then John notices what's missing. "I saw no temple in the city, for its temple is the Lord God the Almighty and the Lamb." No temple. In every other vision of God's presence in Scripture—the tabernacle, Solomon's temple, the heavenly throne room—there was always a sacred building, a holy space set apart. Not here. The whole city is the temple. Every street is holy ground. Every moment is worship. There is no "sacred" and "secular" anymore because everything is filled with God.

"And the city has no need of sun or moon to shine on it, for the glory of God gives it light, and its lamp is the Lamb." The nations walk by that light. Kings bring their glory into the city. The gates never shut—there is no night, no danger, nothing to fear. Everything good and beautiful that human cultures have ever produced, purged of corruption, is brought into the city as an offering to God. Creation isn't destroyed. It's redeemed.

THE RIVER AND THE TREE

John's final vision moves to the heart of the city—and what he sees takes us all the way back to the first pages of the Bible. "Then the angel showed me the river of the water of life, bright as crystal, flowing from the throne of God and of the Lamb through the middle of the street of the city."

A river of life, flowing from God's throne. In Eden, a river watered the garden. In Ezekiel's vision, a river flowed from the temple and brought life wherever it went. Now the source isn't a garden or a building—it's God himself. Endless, crystal-clear, life-giving water flowing forever from the presence of the Creator.

And on each side of the river grows the tree of life. The one from Eden. The one humanity was barred from after the fall, when an angel with a flaming sword stood guard so that no sinful human could reach it. That barrier is gone now. The sword is sheathed. The way is open. The tree bears twelve kinds of fruit, yielding its crop every month—abundance without end, variety without exhaustion. And its leaves are "for the healing of the nations." Not because the nations are still sick, but because in the new creation, everything flourishes. Health is permanent. Wholeness is the atmosphere.

Then comes the sentence that undoes the oldest wound in the Bible: "No longer will there be anything accursed." The curse of Genesis 3—the thorns, the sweat, the pain, the exile, the death—is gone. Completely, permanently gone. What Adam lost, the Lamb restored. What sin broke, grace rebuilt. The story that began with humanity driven out of God's presence ends with humanity living in God's presence forever.

"The throne of God and of the Lamb will be in it, and his servants will worship him. They will see his face, and his name will be on their foreheads." They will see his face. Moses asked to see God's face and was told no one could see it and live. Now, in the new creation, every believer sees it. The deepest longing of the human heart—to know God and be fully known by him—is satisfied. His name on their foreheads means they belong to him completely: known, loved, claimed, and secure.

"And night will be no more. They will need no light of lamp or sun, for the Lord God will be their light, and they will reign forever and ever." They will reign. Not as spectators floating through eternity with nothing to do, but as partners in God's restored creation. Humanity was made to rule the world under God's loving authority. Sin wrecked that vocation. The Lamb restores it. In the new creation, God's people don't just live—they reign. Purposeful. Creative. Active. Alive—in the deepest sense of the word—forever.

COME

The book closes with urgency and invitation. Jesus speaks: "Behold, I am coming soon." He says it three times in these final verses. The promise isn't just about a future event. It's the heartbeat of the church's hope. The Lamb isn't gone. He's coming. And "soon" in God's vocabulary doesn't mean "eventually, maybe." It means "certainly, and closer than you think."

John falls at the angel's feet to worship—and once again the angel stops him. "Worship God." Even at the end of the most spectacular vision in history, the rule is unchanged: worship belongs to God alone. Not to angels. Not to experiences. Not to knowledge about the future. Only to the Lamb.

Then comes the most beautiful invitation in the Bible: "The Spirit and the Bride say, 'Come.' And let the one who hears say, 'Come.' And let the one who is thirsty come; let the one who desires take the water of life without price." The Spirit of God and the church speak together with one voice: Come. That's the final word of God's mission—not a threat, not a lecture, not a deadline. An invitation. The door is still open. The water is still free. Anyone who is thirsty—anyone who knows that the world's golden cups have left them empty—can come and drink.

And John, speaking for every believer who has ever waited, who has ever cried "How long?", who has ever held on to faith when the world seemed to be winning, responds:

"Amen. Come, Lord Jesus!"

The last verse is a benediction: "The grace of the Lord Jesus be with all. Amen." The Bible ends the way it lived—with grace. The same grace that created the world, the same grace that called Abraham, the same grace that sent Jesus to the cross, the same grace that sustained the seven churches, the same grace that carried every martyr home—that grace is the final word. Not judgment. Not fear. Grace.

WHAT THIS MEANS FOR US

First, God's plan is renewal, not destruction. The Bible doesn't end with the world blowing up. It ends with the world being healed. The Christian hope isn't to escape creation but to see it restored. Every good thing—beauty, friendship, creativity, laughter, love—finds its fullest expression in the new creation. What matters to God now will matter forever.

Second, God's presence is the point. The new Jerusalem has no temple because God himself is the temple. The city has no sun because God himself is the light. Every other gift in the new creation—the river, the tree, the streets of gold—is an overflow of one central reality: God is there. And that is enough.

Third, the curse is undone. Every consequence of Genesis 3—death, pain, exile, thorns, tears, broken relationships—is reversed. The Lamb didn't just forgive sin. He healed everything sin damaged. The story of the Bible isn't "paradise lost." It's "paradise restored—and then some."

Fourth, the invitation is still open. The Bible doesn't end with a locked gate. It ends with "Come." The water of life is free. The door is open. The Lamb invites everyone who is thirsty to drink. If you've read this whole book and feel that pull—that thirst for something the world's golden cups can't satisfy—the response is simple: Come.

TALKING POINTS

1. **The "new" heaven and earth isn't a replacement—it's a renewal.** Why does that distinction matter for how we think about creation and the future?

2. **The new Jerusalem is shaped like a perfect cube—the same shape as the Holy of Holies.** What does it mean that the whole city is now the Most Holy Place?

3. **There is no temple and no sun in the new creation.** What do those absences tell us about what God's presence really means?

4. **The tree of life reappears for the first time since Genesis 3.** How does this ending connect to the Bible's beginning? What has changed?

5. John's response to everything he's seen is four words: "Amen. Come, Lord Jesus!" If you could sum up your response to Revelation in one sentence, what would it be?

The story is finished. The dragon is destroyed. The beasts are gone. Babylon is silent. Death is dead. And in their place stands a city of light, a river of life, a tree that never stops bearing fruit, and a God who has finally, fully, permanently come home to his people.

The Lamb reigns. The Bride is ready. The gates are open. The invitation stands.

Come.

www.ingramcontent.com/pod-product-compliance
Lightning Source LLC
Chambersburg PA
CBHW050957050726
47592CB00007B/2609